THAT DAY IN DALLAS

Also By Richard B. Trask

Salem Village and the Witch Hysteria (1975, Revised 1991)
As the Century Turned (Co-authored, 1989)
The Devil Hath Been Raised (1992, Revised 1997)
Pictures of the Pain: Photography and the Assassination of President Kennedy (1994)
Photographic Memory (1996)
Danvers, Massachusetts from 1850 through 1899 (1996)
A Hearty Band of Firefighters (Introduction, co-edited 1997)

THAT DAY IN DALLAS

THREE PHOTOGRAPHERS CAPTURE ON FILM
THE DAY PRESIDENT KENNEDY DIED

By
Richard B. Trask

Yeoman Press
Danvers, Massachusetts

Publisher's Cataloguing-in-Publication Data

Trask, Richard Barry, 1947 –
    That day in Dallas: three photographers capture on film the day President Kennedy died/Richard B. Trask.
        136 p.   28 cm.
    1. Altgens, James William, 1919-1995.
    2. Kennedy, John F. (John Fitzgerald), 1917-1963 – Assassination.
    3. Kennedy, John F. (John Fitzgerald), 1917-1963 – Portraits, caricatures, etc.
    4. Murray, James Patrick, 1929-
    5. Stoughton, Cecil William, 1920-
    I. Title.

Library of Congress Catalogue Card Number: 97-61937
ISBN 0-9638595-2-8
E842.9   364.1

Photograph credits appear on page *vi*

For information, address:
Yeoman Press
35 Centre Street
Danvers, MA 01923

Printed in the United States of America
1 3 5 7 9 10 8 6 4 2

Contents

Dedication

To Jim Murray, Cecil Stoughton, Jim Altgens, Charles Bronson and Phil Willis. These recorders of history have not only shared their memories and photographs with me, but also their friendship.

Acknowledgments

Grateful acknowledgment is made to the many people who have assisted me in my researching and producing this volume. As ever, Ethel Trask, my wife, best friend and now publishing partner, has allowed me the opportunity to pursue my interests and the support and technological knowledge to put those interests into concrete form.

To the photographers and their families who gave me the gift of their knowledge and remembrances of the events, including: Cecil W. Stoughton; Jim Murray; James P. Altgens; William Allen; Frank Cancellare; Thomas Atkins; Tom C. Dillard; Robert H. Jackson, Donald C. Grant; Philip L. and Marilyn S. Willis; and Jimmy Darnell.

To the researchers who answered my queries, volunteered information and gave advice, including: Vincent Palamara; John R. Woods, II; Andy Winiarczyk and The Last Hurrah Bookshop of Williamsport, PA; Jerry D. Rose, editor of *The Fourth Decade* of Fredonia, New York; Jerry Organ; Dennis Ford; W. Anthony Marsh; Todd Wayne Vaughan; Harrison E. Livingstone; Tom Jones, publisher of the *Kennedy Assassination Chronicles* of Grand Prairie, Texas; Mark A. Oakes; and Martin Shackelford.

To the archivists, librarians and photographers who gave me research and technical assistance and picture sources, including: John Walker Studio, Dallas, Texas; AP/Wide World Photos and Lisa Nelson; Archivist Gary Mack and The Sixth Floor Museum at Dealey Plaza, Dallas, Texas; Archivist Evelyn Salz of Western New England College, Springfield, Massachusetts; Producer Mary Mapes and News Anchor Dan Rather of CBS News; members and staff of the Assassination Records Review Board; the staff of the Peabody Institute Library of Danvers, Massachusetts; the Dallas Public Library Texas/Dallas Collection; the Audio-Visual Department and Archive Aid Donna Cotterell of the John F. Kennedy Library, Boston, Massachusetts; and Audiovisual Archivist E. Philip Scott and Archivist Allen Fisher of the Lyndon B. Johnson Library, Austin, Texas. These people, in large and small measure, assisted me in the research and producing of this work, and I thank them for their kindnesses.

Photo Credits

The photographs in this volume, many copyrighted, were either taken by the following individuals or repose in the following collections: John F. Kennedy Library, front cover, p. 11, 16-22, 24-29, 31, 33, 53-54; Cecil W. Stoughton, p.13, 36-37, 39-44, 50 bottom; Jimmy Darnell, p. 34 top; Tom C. Dillard, p. 34 bottom; Joe Laird, p. 38; L. B. J. Library Collection – Cecil Stoughton, p. 46-47, 49, 50 top; James W. Altgens, p. 57-59, 60 bottom, 62 top, 66; Richard O. Bothun, p. 60 top, 63 top, 68 bottom; AP/WIDE WORLD PHOTOS., p. 61, 62 bottom, 63 bottom, 64, 67, 68 top, 72, 73 left; Donald C. "Clint" Grant, p. 69; Copyright © Robert H. Jackson, from the collections of the Texas/Dallas History and Archives Division, Dallas Public Library, p. 73 top; National Archives, p. 73 bottom; Jim Murray, p. 77; Copyright © Jim Murray Film. All Rights Reserved., p. 81-88, 90-91, 93-95, 97-101, 102 top, 103-104, 105 bottom, 106-107, 109-112, 115-118, 120-124, 127, 129, back cover; Copyright © 1978 Phil Willis, All Rights Reserved., p. 79, 96; William Allen, p. 89; A. J. L'Hoste, p. 102 bottom; Ernest C. Mentesana, p. 105 top; *Dallas Morning News*, p. 125.

Introduction

In 1994 my wife Ethel and I self-published a 640-page hardcover book titled, *Pictures of the Pain: Photography and the Assassination of President Kennedy*. This work was the result of 10 years of study into the history of the photography of the murder of President John F. Kennedy on November 22, 1963. It had been my intent to gather into that volume as much information about the photographers and cameramen, both professional and amateur, who recorded the last few minutes in the life of the 35th President of the United States, the serious wounding of the Governor of Texas and the confused aftermath at the shooting site in Dallas, Texas.

During my decade of research, I had located and interviewed several score of these assassination picture-takers, many of whose recollections had never before been published or even gathered. In the book I recounted the story of how these people's films and photos were used and sometimes abused by the various government investigations into the shooting, by the print and electronic media and by the various critics of the government investigations. Peppered throughout the text were over 300 illustrations, approximately 40% of them never before having been published. The nature of the book, however, was that of text augmented by photographs, with even the largest illustrations limited by the 7" x 9" page layout space. I kept the thought that someday it might be worthwhile to publish some of the best of this photography in a larger illustrated format and on quality paper.

A number of the Dealey Plaza assassination scene photographers had, as a result of my research visits and frequent communications, become comfortable enough with me and the objectivity and sincerity of my project to share personal recollections and photographs seldom shared with anyone. Three professional still photographers who were there in 1963, and with whom I became particularly friendly, had each taken from his own unique perspective a number of photos which collectively covered almost all the events in Texas relating to the assassination story. In addition, several of these photographers' pictures, due to their historical content, technical quality and broad media distribution, have become indelible images by which history and we will forever recall the sad events in Dallas.

Cecil W. Stoughton was official White House photographer. The nature of his job gave him unique access to the President. The photos he made of the swearing-in of President Lyndon Johnson aboard *Air Force One* after President Kennedy had been pronounced dead, are the only images recorded of that event. As an insider, his closeness to the subject gives us an intimate look at the final day of the John Kennedy presidency and of the somber genesis of the Johnson administration.

James P. Altgens was a native Dallasite who worked for the mammoth Associated Press news-gathering organization. On his own initiative Altgens had chosen a photo site that Friday morning where no other professional photographer ventured. His camera skills and prior planning gave the world crisp and clear photographs of the ill-fated motorcade before the horror, as well as dramatic images of the assassination itself.

Jim Murray was a local Dallas free-lance photographer who had not planned on shooting pictures of the Kennedy motorcade. By happenstance he was in Dealey Plaza at the time of the assassination. Rushing to his car and grabbing his two cameras to record what he initially thought was merely an embarrassing incident involving teenagers and fire-crackers, Murray stayed with the story from that moment until Monday after-noon. Though he did not photograph the assassination itself, through native instinct and knowledge of the local scene, he recorded more of the story than any other single photographer. His independence and initiative allowed him to document the numerous assassination-related Dallas scenes in real time, including accused assassin Lee Harvey Oswald held in police custody.

Among the photographs made by each of these professional photographers were several images which would later spawn heated controversy. Upon the death of accused assassin Lee Oswald on Sun-day, November 24, 1963, questions quickly arose concerning his actual in-volvement and the possible involvement of others in an assassination conspiracy. Almost every fact, piece of evidence, or seemingly odd occurrence became fuel for conspiratorial speculation by an emerging group of independent researchers, assassi-nation buffs and quick-to-print authors.

Photographic documentation of the assassination and related pre- and post-event images were pored over by amateur sleuths looking to find elusive truths from within these images' emul-sions. Though government investigators soon lost interest in studying the photog-raphy of the event, many of the loosely knit assassination research community, acknowledging the slice of reality inherent in photography, found or thought they found or convinced themselves they found evidences of conspiracy.

We shall briefly examine the circumstances relating to several contro-versial photographs taken by these three professional photographers to see in these particular cases the substance of such speculation and photo interpretation.

The volume before you does not record the entire story of the assassina-tion. Nor is this the story of Lee Oswald, Jack Ruby or the murder of Dallas police officer J. D. Tippet. Rather, this is an illustrated recounting of the experiences of three professional photographers as they lived the events of November 22, 1963, and of the technical, emotional and professional manner in which they at-tempted to cover the biggest, most impor-tant news story of their careers.

In this volume I am pleased to present individual chapters about these three photographers. Each chapter has been revised and enlarged from my origi-nal book. Of particular interest should be the over 110 large-format images taken by these men of the 1963 assassination events. I have consistently attempted to obtain and publish clear, original or first-generation prints, and to reproduce the entire image as shot by the photographer, believing that these are the most truthful and accurate representations of the reality of what the photographers experienced. Where possible I have also selected images previously unpublished.

The skill of these three photogra-phers and their ability to locate them-selves at the right place at the right time allows us to experience as close to first-hand as possible one of the seminal events of 20th century history. On that day in Dallas, American history was changed forever.

Richard B. Trask

CHAPTER I

The White House Photographer

It had the feel of a typical motorcade procession, as typical, that is, as a motorcade can be when you are traveling along with the President of the United States. Cecil Stoughton had been in numerous such processions during the last 35 months. As official White House photographer and a captain in the United States Army, Stoughton had made over 8,000 pictures of events surrounding the activities of President John Fitzgerald Kennedy and the First Family.[1]

During the last two days, Stoughton had taken dozens of pictures of the President's much-publicized autumn 1963 visit to Texas. He had made exposures of the President and his lovely wife being greeted by numerous dignitaries, special groups, and hordes of common people, many who would hopefully also be Kennedy supporters in the upcoming presidential election of 1964. This was Stoughton's fifth motorcade of the Texas trip, and it did not seem noticeably different from similar receptions the day before at Houston, and San Antonio, and at Fort Worth.

Some of the news people traveling along with the presidential party appeared to want to make more of the fact that this was Dallas – a town possessing a rough right-wing reputation. But Stoughton did not discern anything in the airport reception crowd that indicated hostility towards the President. If anything, the crowd along the route looked larger than in previous motorcades.

It was near the end of the downtown motorcade procession. The open Chevrolet convertible reserved for the still photographers and positioned as the seventh car behind the President's vehicle was preparing to make a sharp left turn on a street adjacent to a small park when Stoughton heard three loud reports. He turned to his left to LIFE magazine staff photographer Art Rickerby and exclaimed, "Boy! These Texans know how to welcome a guy, don't they?" In his mind he visualized a Texas cowboy wearing a ten-gallon hat standing on a rooftop and waving a six-shooter, while firing it into the sky.[2] Confused reality quickly replaced images of local color. Stoughton, though he could not as yet comprehend it, was for the next few hours not working for his now former President, nor for the United States Army. Rather, beyond any pedantic, immediate, political, or souvenir photographic consideration, he was working, now more than at any time in his career, for the historical record. American presidential history had just taken an oblique turn, not as a result of the ballots of millions of people that Kennedy had been spending so great an effort in wooing, but by the obscene blasts of the barrel of a rifle.

~

Cecil William Stoughton was born in Oskaloosa, Iowa, on January 18, 1920, and at the age of 20 had enlisted in the Army Air Corps seeking a possible photographic career. After war broke out in 1941, he was sent to a LIFE magazine photographic training course, and was assigned to the 13th Air Force. Headquartered at Guadalcanal, the unit was commanded by one of Hollywood's academy award winning directors, Frank Lloyd. Stoughton worked in both motion picture and still photography in the South Pacific theater of operations during the war, and by 1947 he had determined to make a career of photography in the armed forces. Assigned to Military Air Transport Service, Stoughton served in Hawaii until 1951, when he was reassigned as a motion picture cameraman to the Joint Chiefs of Staff, under the supervision of the Office of the Secretary of Defense. In 1954 he sailed on the shake-down cruise of the first nuclear-powered submarine, the *USS Nautilus*, and in 1957 he traded his Air Force sergeant's stripes for a direct commission as a first lieutenant in the Army Signal Corps as an officer-photographer. In 1958 General Chester V. "Ted" Clifton, Deputy Chief of Information of the Army, needed a photographer for Army Missile Command special assignments, and Stoughton was selected to become photographic officer at Huntsville, Alabama. As part of his assignment Stoughton photographed significant U.S. satellite launches at Cape Canaveral, Florida, including *Pioneer I* on October 11, 1958. Through 1959 he continued to serve as Army photographer at Cape Canaveral.[3]

By late 1960 Stoughton was working under Major General Clifton at the Pentagon in Washington and was assigned to take pictures of President-elect Kennedy's inauguration. Stoughton had photographed previous presidential inaugurations, and knew where some of the Capitol building's best vantage points were located. On Inauguration Day, January 20, 1961, Stoughton, using his own initiative, worked his way up to a good spot on the inaugural stand and managed to make a photo of President Kennedy showing a full-face image while using a standard, non-telephoto camera lens. General Clifton, who had been appointed military aide to the President, was impressed with Stoughton's photos and showed them to Kennedy, who was also impressed. Clifton suggested to the President that it might be a good idea to have this photographer available to the White House.[4]

Prior to this time, there had never been an "in-house" photographer specifically assigned to the President. Clifton's suggestion of such an inside photographer who would be at the beck and call of the White House, could provide all sorts of souvenir and historical record photographs and, due to the nature of the work, would not be competitive with the press photographers, seemed an attractive idea. Positive results from such a White House photographer could only add to General Clifton's

standing with the President, and if perchance the photographer screwed up, as Stoughton would later wryly comment, "I'd be in Guam tomorrow."[5]

As the weeks passed following Stoughton's new assignment, the White House staff became more familiar with one another. Stoughton's office was right underneath the President's, and he arranged with the President's secretary, Mrs. Evelyn Lincoln, to have a buzzer hooked up to his basement desk, so that when a picture was needed or an opportunity presented itself, Stoughton could be alerted. The staff also began tipping him off about various developments. After a while, recalls Stoughton, "I became such a part of the scene, that many times I didn't even need a telephoto lens. I was close enough just to take pictures normally. And they expected it."[6]

The value of a presidential photographer from a branch of the military service had not been lost on White House Navy Aide, Captain Tazewell Shepard. Navy photographer Robert L. Knudsen had previously performed White House photo assignments from the time of President Truman. He was assigned a regular slot at the Kennedy White House. In early 1963 the Navy provided an additional photographer, Thomas M. Atkins, to almost exclusively perform motion picture work. This inter-service military aide rivalry never bothered the photographers personally, as they got along well, and often found themselves assigned to the same event. Shades of one-upmanship were evident on occasion, however. Stoughton would often cover the visit of an important dignitary, making pictures of the VIP's activities, which at the end of the visit would be presented to the dignitary by the State Department in a remembrance album. When Navy cameraman Atkins was assigned to the White House, part of his duty was to make color movies of such visits, presenting an edited film to the departing guest, and on occasion a new projector to go along with the movie film.[7]

Captain Stoughton was on call to make pictures of whatever the President did

White House photographers Cecil Stoughton (right) and Robert Knudsen pose for a picture off Newport, Rhode Island, on September 22, 1962. Stoughton holds a 16mm movie camera while his 35mm Alpa hangs from his neck.

that required photography for the record or simply to be provided as cherished mementos for a visitor to the Oval Office. Wherever the President went during regular work schedules or on weekend vacations to Hyannis, Massachusetts, or Palm Beach, Florida, the working press would follow, and Stoughton would often go for historical documentation. He recalls that the President and his wife "were good about not using me in times when it was unnecessary. They weren't just frivolous assignments. I'd get a call once or twice at home to come

in and do something that hadn't been thought of prior to that, but that was no problem."[8]

Never becoming personally familiar with his Commander-in-Chief, Stoughton nevertheless became a devoted member of the President's team. He often had closer access to the First Family than most of the staff, but he did his work as unobtrusively as possible. He shot his pictures fast, knowing that Kennedy would usually only stand still for a couple of shots, before going off in a different direction. He also quickly learned that the President's nod or a particular glance in Stoughton's direction meant that time was up.[9]

During official presidential sojourns out of the White House, Stoughton did not have 100 percent access to the President or the event. His position during these trips was looked upon as being part of the press package. Stoughton would ride with the press in their plane or in a press car within a motorcade. At speeches and other stationary events, Stoughton soon became familiar with and friendly towards many of the Secret Service agents, so that he was recognized as no threat and could be about his job without any fuss. Stoughton remembers many of the agents as his buddies. He often helped out the working photographers by getting the agents to let the photographers come up one at a time and take pictures in what was often a restricted area.[10]

Stoughton's face was often captured in press photos due to the nature of his job. "My job was for the most part to show where the President was, where they were, whom they were with, and what they were doing – not just pictures of their faces. Mrs. Kennedy often said, 'We know what we look like, we don't want pictures of us, show us where we are.' In other words, get behind us. So I'm behind in a lot of pictures."[11]

Stoughton's access to the President was not always consistent. Unlike later assignments with President Johnson, and with the normal procedures of later presidential photographers who are almost constantly near their subject, during tours Stoughton often had to scramble along with the other press photographers. "And then when we'd go the weekends to Hyannis, I would have access all day Saturday and Sunday, and my buddies would hire a boat and try to see him with long lenses from a rocking boat. And I'm on the *Honey Fitz* [boat] with him. But they knew that and didn't object because I didn't do anything with the pictures. I didn't give them to AP and UPI."[12]

Stoughton's favorite sequence of presidential pictures taken during his career occurred in October 1962, when the President's children Caroline and John-John made one of their frequent visits to their father in the Oval Office. Recalls Stoughton, "I heard the President clapping and singing out, 'Hey, Here's John-John.' " Stoughton was at the door, and the President signaled for him to come in. Within three minutes Stoughton had squeezed off twelve pictures recording the President playing with his children. After they were processed, Stoughton brought them to Kennedy. The President chose one, and summoning Press Secretary Pierre Salinger told him that particular picture should be released to the press who were always clamoring for such an informal family photo. With that, for one rare occasion a Stoughton picture was distributed to the press and was published around the world.

Later Stoughton requested the President to autograph a copy of this picture, Kennedy inscribing, "For Captain Stoughton, who captured beautifully a happy moment at the White House. John F. Kennedy."[13]

The mainstay of Stoughton's photographic equipment were two cameras – a Swiss-made Alpa Reflex and a 500C Hasselblad. The Alpa Reflex was a 35mm SLR, usually used along with a wide-angle 35mm or a 180mm telephoto lens. Stoughton's favorite, however, was the Hasselblad. "The Hasselblad was my tool, an extension of my right arm. I used it every chance I got. Hasselblad was a magazine camera with interchangeable magazines. You would put black-and-white in one, color in one, transparency film in one." The camera bodies were Army property, although some of his interchangeable lenses were borrowed, including a newly introduced 50mm, which Stoughton obtained from the Hasselblad people in late 1963. An 80mm and 150mm lens were also used on a regular basis, and Stoughton shot his 120 film into a 12-frame sequence, using the Hasselblad magazine. Stoughton would use the type of film most

One of President Kennedy's and Cecil Stoughton's favorite photos was this candid shot made in the White House Oval Office in October 1962 of the President and his two children. President Kennedy inscribed a copy of the photograph to Captain Stoughton.

appropriate to the occasion. "If it was a colorful event, well, I'd use color. But a lot of times black-and-white was appropriate and adequate."[14]

Although Stoughton was an in-house staff member, neither his photo lab, nor photo archive, was located within the White House. At this time there was no photographic department at the White House, and although most staff understood the concept of photographic documentation for the record, the function was still under the Army or Naval Aide's wing. The immediate use of the photographs was often for the expedient objective of politics, good will, and campaign pictures, without specific forethought of future archival use. As Stoughton remembers, "If there were

something somebody wanted or had a need for, I would make a batch of prints and pass them around – give them to the various people."

Whereas Stoughton processed his own film for 16 years while in the Air Force, he did less and less while an officer, as the military "didn't like officers running around doing that kind of stuff. They have people who will do it for you." By the end of his stint at the White House in 1965 during the Johnson administration, then Major Stoughton was an e\xception, actually photographing and going on trips. Back in the early days of the Kennedy administration, however, Stoughton sent his film over to the Pentagon for developing. As time went on and as several technicians were assigned to Stoughton, they built a darkroom at a location within a former brewery, and later still during the Johnson administration, a color facility was set up on M Street in Georgetown.[15]

Turnaround time for pictures was quite fast. Shots taken in the morning could be proofed by the afternoon with enlargements the next day. Remembering the early operation as "kind of loose," Stoughton recalls that contact sheets were seldom made. "I usually got just a selection of the best – have the guy in the lab select the best pictures technically, sharp and all that, and send them up . . . I wasn't as well prepared for the mechanical type stuff, as I was being busy taking pictures. I let somebody else worry about the details."[16]

Most of the Kennedy White House photographic materials are now located and preserved at the John F. Kennedy Library in Boston. What is quite evident is that in the working White House during the Kennedy administration no one was responsible nor concerned about the archival nature of the films other than a vague understanding that they would some day be historically valuable. The chief concern was day-to-day operations. Photographer Robert Knudsen "was told specifically not to make contact prints of his rolls, no one at the White House wanted to bother with them, and instead to print each negative frame in 5" x 7" for the files and for viewing by the White House Staff."[17]

Stoughton's numbering system for his rolls of film was numerical, beginning each calendar year with the first assignment. An assignment could be anywhere from 1 to 95 negatives depending upon the occasion, and included a prefix "C" if it was done in color. As Kennedy Library Audio-Visual Archivist Allan Goodrich explained it, "The numbering system with each assignment is simply a numerical listing as the negative was printed and/or identified by Stoughton after his films were processed and printed. No attempt was made by either Stoughton or his lab to keep the film frames in numerical sequence as they had been in the roll, or to keep them

serially numbered according to day or time."[18] Stoughton confirms this procedure remarking, "I had a technician at the lab who, after the negatives were processed, would put a number on them so we could find them, and it was rather loose. Whatever roll the person was processing at the time would be the first number."[19]

In 1963 Stoughton was given an additional assignment area. "I started in the movie business in 1963 when the President went to Europe, and Jackie was pregnant and didn't go. She charged me with the responsibility of covering his trip so she could see what he did while he was gone. When I came back I had 3,600 feet of Kodachrome to which I attached sound, and some of his speeches and crowd noise and music. I showed it on the Fourth of July weekend in 1963. I showed it three times. He wanted to see what he did. From then on I did a lot of weekend filming, at the Cape and the last weekend they were together in Virginia in November."[20]

Stoughton had made some personal family shots of the First Family at their farm at Wexford in Atoka, Virginia, including a funny sequence of a horse nosing a sitting and relaxed President for a sugar cube. This is the "last weekend" to which Stoughton refers.

Twenty years after the events, Stoughton would recount on ABC's *Good Morning America* television show his one-man multi-media process. "I'd have three cameras around my neck on straps and a 16mm movie camera in my hand, and I'd squirt off a few feet of movies and I'd take a couple of stills. So I would have both kinds of records, because we were talking about history. And Mrs. Kennedy would like to have the fact that they were living in the White House recorded. . . ."[21]

In the fall of 1963 Kennedy's approval rating with the American public was, according to a Gallup Poll, at 59%, having fallen due in part to many displeased with his civil rights stance. Kennedy had decided in light of the 1964 presidential election, that he should visit the South in order to boost his image. The states of Florida and Texas, so crucial during his 1960 campaign, were targeted. Then serving Texas Governor John B. Connally would state 15 years later before the House Select Committee on Assassinations his belief that Kennedy had requested the five-city Texas visit in order to raise campaign money and to enhance his political position in Texas.[22]

Any time the President journeys outside of the Washington area the event initiates hundreds of hours of pre-planning and dozens of personnel being put to work on logistics. Political advance men would make contacts and arrangements for events, meetings, and speeches, while security, transportation, and communication coordinators would handle their numerous tasks. Like the many other military and governmental employees, as well as political aides who would be needed to fulfill various functions in a presidential journey, Cecil Stoughton was informed that he would be making the trip and began to put his professional gear and personal wardrobe together. As was typically the case, Stoughton, like the other assigned White House military photographers, did not wear his uniform on such trips. He would wear a civilian suit in order not to draw undue attention and comment. Robert Knudsen would not be going on the Texas trip due to treatment for metal slivers in his eye. Tom Atkins would go. His assignment was to film the trip highlights with a 16mm movie camera using color film. As usual, Stoughton brought with him his favorite camera, the Hasselblad, together with his 35mm Alpa Reflex.

On Wednesday evening, November 20, 1963, Stoughton had been on duty to record the formal presidential reception at the White House for the Justices of the United States Supreme Court. During the morning of November 21, he had been called in to photograph the President's meeting with the U. S. Ambassadors to Upper Volta and Gabon.

At about 11 a.m. on November 21, the President and his entourage left Andrews Air Force Base for Texas, and Stoughton's photo technicians would later log the photographic sequences of the Texas trip as "C420" for the color pictures, and "525" for the black-and-white photo series. During the next 24 hours Stoughton would make a number of pictures of the President's activities including receptions at San Antonio, Brooks Medical Center, Kelly Air Field, a Latin-American citizens' group at the Rice Hotel in Houston, and a testimonial dinner for Congressman Albert Thomas at the Houston Coliseum.

It was just before midnight on November 21 that the Kennedy motorcade arrived at the Hotel Texas in Fort Worth following a 10-hour whirlwind schedule. Overnight arrangements had been made for the trip by the advance team, and as was typical, the military personnel would sleep two to a room. This night Stoughton was assigned room 804 on the same floor as the President, sharing accommodations, as he sometimes did, with Warrant Officer Ira D. Gearhart. Gearhart was required to travel close to the President while being as inconspicuous as possible, all the time carrying a 30-pound metal suitcase. Often known by the popular euphemism as "the bag man," Gearhart kept in his mind the combination to the suitcase. This suitcase contained codes the President could use in case of nuclear attack in order to launch the United States stockpile of missiles. Also included within the case were documents containing retaliation options and statistics for the President to consider should it be necessary to go to war with the Soviet Union.[23]

November 22 dawned drizzly, and Stoughton's first assignment of the day would be to record the speech the President was to make in the parking lot across 8th Street from Hotel Texas. A soggy, but enthusiastic Fort Worth crowd had been gathering early to get a glimpse of the Kennedys. Cleaning his camera lenses, Stoughton decided the overcast morning would be suitable for black-and-white film, and as his Alpa Reflex was already loaded with fast-speed Tri-X film from yesterday's events, he decided to finish off the 36-exposure roll.

On Friday morning the President emerges from Hotel Texas, greeted by a cordon of cameramen and photographers.

A sea of smiling faces, craned necks and outstretched hands greet the President in the parking lot.

Fort Worth Congressman Jim Wright introduces the dignitaries at the podium including Governor John Connally.

The President delivers a short, energetic address while photographers scramble to record the scene.

Stoughton concentrates on recording the address from several different angles.

Switching his Alpa camera to the vertical plane, Stoughton photographs President Kennedy in mid-sentence. Texas Senator Ralph Yarborough stands behind the President.

At the Hotel Texas Chamber of Commerce breakfast, Mrs. Kennedy, led by Secret Service Agent Clint Hill, makes a late but grand entrance. Stoughton is now using his Hasselblad camera, loaded with color film.

*Vice-President Lyndon Johnson exchanges pleasantries with Mrs. Kennedy at the Chamber of Commerce break-
fast. Lady Bird Johnson looks on at left while the President smiles out toward the audience.*

The First Lady and President walk from the hotel, ready to board a borrowed convertible for the trip to Carswell Air Force Base. A temporary communications antenna and the United States flag have been attached to the front right fender of the car. Secret Service Agent Lem Johns, back to camera, looks to his right.

Stoughton's 17-exposure sequence of the parking lot speech captures President Kennedy walking out of the hotel main entrance at about 8:50 a.m. with Vice-President Lyndon Johnson, local Congressman Jim Wright, and other dignitaries in tow. A cordon of over a dozen still and motion picture cameramen record on film almost identical views of the political procession for later TV and newspaper coverage.

Kennedy is next seen within the Stoughton sequence wading into the outer edge of the crowd, the closest members of whom are stretching out their hands for a shake or touch. Then Stoughton makes seven shots from the side of the flat-bed podium as Congressman Wright introduces those standing on it. Stoughton next moves behind the podium and makes two shots from a perch on a step-ladder. With the back of the President's head and shoulders in the foreground, the pictures show the crowd listening to his words while the photographers in front of them continue to snap away. Coming around to the front of the podium, Stoughton takes three additional shots of the President, two of the photos centering primarily on Kennedy's face. The series is a fine example of Stoughton's using his access to record what the President was doing, whom he was with, and what he saw.[24]

Following the outside public rally, the President was next scheduled to address a Chamber of Commerce breakfast in the hotel. Stoughton positioned himself in the large hotel ballroom now using his Hasselblad 500C loaded with 120 color film. The negative size allowed Stoughton to squeeze off 12 exposures per roll. Stoughton used the 6 left on this roll from yesterday's take to record Mr. Kennedy's arrival, introductions at the podium by Chamber of Commerce President Raymond Buck, and Mrs. Kennedy's late but grand arrival wearing a pink suit with matching pillbox hat. She had last worn this suit during a reception at the White House in October 1962 when Algerian Premier Ahmed Ben Bella was welcomed on a state visit.[25]

Stoughton then records Mrs. Kennedy at the head table and then standing with Vice-President Johnson, both beaming large, natural smiles. The last picture on the roll is of the President at the podium being greeted with applause from those standing at the head table, while the photographers down front shoot the scene. This set of pictures, like many of Stoughton's sequences printed in a small uncropped format, has a candid home snapshot quality about it, much like pictures taken at a wedding reception, the only difference being that Stoughton's includes famous faces and the presidential seal. These are work-a-day pictures of real people.

Changing film, Stoughton, at about 10:30 a.m., makes three shots in front of the Hotel Texas in anticipation of the President leaving for Carswell Air Force Base and the short flight to Dallas. The morning had transformed from gray and drizzly to a cloudless and blue sky. In front of the hotel Governor John Connally, wearing a white Stetson, is seen conferring with chain smoking White House Assistant Press Secretary Malcolm Kilduff. In another photograph presidential aides Larry O'Brien and Dave Powers are on the sidewalk in front of the hotel while a TV crew from Channel 11 awaits to broadcast the President's departure. Finally Mr. and Mrs. Kennedy emerge from the hotel making straight for the white convertible with red interior being used in Fort Worth as the presidential limousine.[26]

The motorcade through downtown Fort Worth is recorded in two Stoughton photos taken from a moving convertible and looking forward at the motorcade to the front and the crowds on the sides. On the Texas trip, as was highly unusual, both the President and the Vice-President rode in the motorcade, though never in the same car. The presidential limousine was trailed by a Secret Service follow-up car, then the Vice-President with his own follow-up vehicle.

The motorcade in Fort Worth

Directly behind the Vice-President's follow-up car trailed the White House print press car, which carried the Press Secretary, wireservice reporters, and typically a local press representative. Behind this car would be either the still-picture camera car or the motion picture camera car. During this motorcade Stoughton's still-camera car was directly behind the print press car, and when they arrived in Dallas, their motorcade position would be switched with that of the movie car. Stoughton's shots of the motorcade are made on Main Street, which has been decked out a little early with Christmas decorations featuring Santa Clauses and garland rings spanning the streets. The second shot is taken with a view of the President's limousine five car lengths ahead as it makes a right turn in front of the 1894 Tarrant County Courthouse. President Kennedy stands to acknowledge the band playing on the front steps.[27]

During such motorcades the President would sometimes see a homemade sign, or a small group of people who would strike his eye, and he would tell the Secret Service driver to stop the car so that he could greet them. After a few moments amidst the excited crowd, the car would continue on. Upon such impromptu stops some cameramen would instinctively jump out of their convertibles to make that potential "good picture." Often they would not reach the action before the motorcade started up again, and would be forced to jump for their ride. On several occasions while Stoughton was traveling in such motorcades, he would also get caught in the dash for a picture, but unlike his press colleagues, a few times he was able to catch a ride on the foot jump on the rear of the presidential Lincoln, holding on to the handles attached to the trunk. At the next stop he would get off and go back to his own car. The Secret Service did not object to this occasional foray on the Lincoln, for Stoughton was a safe buffer. Both the security men and Stoughton, however, were well aware of the President's disdain for anyone to ride too often or too long at this position, which obscured the President from the people and might look too much like overprotection.[28]

Arriving at Carswell Air Force Base, the President and his manifest of guests boarded the 707 jet designated *Air Force One*. Stoughton, did not ride in the President's plane, but instead was a passenger in the press plane. During the ridiculously brief 13-minute flight to Dallas's Love Field, the press plane was allowed to arrive first, so that they would be ready to record the grand arrival of *Air Force One*.

Stoughton recalls that the press expected a hostile atmosphere in conservative Dallas, but that "it sure didn't spin off into the Love Field crowd. My pictures show dozens of flags, hand-painted welcome signs, a lot of warmth. . . . I did not feel nor see any hostility, certainly not during the whole time we were there." Stoughton later recalled the scene as "just a beautiful reception, a bright, warm, sunny day and thousands of people cheering – screaming like they had at Fort Worth, Houston and San Antonio."[29]

Still working with his Hasselblad, Stoughton captures the President and First Lady walking down the gangway off *Air Force One*.

With thousands of enthusiastic spectators cheering, the elegant First Couple walk down the gangway at Dallas's Love Field.

Stoughton captures a detail-rich view of the airport reception from the Air Force One *hatch. The Kennedys and Johnsons are plying through the VIP reception line, while the press observe from the closest horizontal line. The public wait for a glimpse behind a chain link fence at the rear.*

NBC cameraman Dave Wiegman (in hat) and CBS cameraman Tom Craven (to the left of Wiegman) are among the numerous media on hand to record the airport reception. Mrs. Kennedy cradles red roses given her moments earlier by the Mayor's wife.

President Kennedy works the crowd, his efforts recorded by numerous cameramen. Following President Kennedy at his right rear is Assistant Special Agent-In-Charge Roy H. Kellerman. In the extreme right background Vice-President Johnson is also walking the fence greeting spectators.

Mrs. Kennedy walks the chain-link fence line, greeting excited Texans. She now includes among the red roses a gift bouquet of white asters. A smiling LIFE *magazine correspondent Hugh Sidey trails behind, observing the impromptu reception line.*

Upon reaching the tarmac, Mrs. Kennedy is presented with a beautiful bouquet of red roses by Mrs. Earle Cabell, wife of the Dallas mayor. After making a picture of this scene, Stoughton scurries up the gangway to shoot a view of the reception line with the large and enthusiastic crowd of spectators to its rear behind a chain link fence. Quickly returning to the tarmac, Stoughton captures shots of the President and Mrs. Kennedy greeting others in the receiving line, including 85-year-old loyal Democrat Annie S. Dunbar, who is seated in a wheelchair.[30]

Now out of film, Stoughton reloads the magazine. The President and First Lady, seeing the exuberance of the public, veer into the crowd of obviously friendly supporters located on the opposite side of a chest-high chain-link fence. Stoughton records two frames showing the Kennedys working their way along the fence as they briefly greet and touch the numerous outstretched hands of the delighted spectators. Mrs. Kennedy's Secret Service guard, Clint Hill, stays nearby.

Stoughton temporarily leaves the fence area trying to locate a better shooting position. While on the move, he takes a shot of presidential aides Dave Powers and Kenny O'Donnell positioned in the jump seat of the Cadillac Secret Service follow-up car. Powers has in his hand a movie camera with which he often took souvenir home movies of the President and the crowd's reaction to him.[31]

Recollects Stoughton, "I stood upon a cement foundation of a lamp, about two feet high, and that gave me a chance to look down instead of fighting everybody else's head. And they walked right by me, and that was the last time I made a picture of them. They were just an arm's length away. They got into the car within a couple seconds after that and drove into town."[32]

The custom-built 1961 presidential Lincoln Continental drop-top convertible sedan was equipped with removable, transparent-plastic roof panels. These so-called bubble-top attachments had been removed for the Dallas motorcade. The motorcade, consisting of about twenty-three vehicles as well as escort motorcycles, was scheduled to wind its way from Love Field through the downtown business district and on to the Dallas Trade Mart, where the President was to give a luncheon address. Those riding in the President's car included Secret Service agent and driver William Greer and Assistant Special Agent-in-Charge Roy Kellerman in the front seat. Texas Governor John B. Connally and his wife, Nellie, were in the right and left jump seats, while President and Mrs. Kennedy were in the rear seat, with the President on the right side.

At about 11:55 a.m. the President's shiny blue-black convertible began to move out. As was typical, the camera people made a scramble for their vehicles. The pace was hectic but routine. Stoughton's car was a convertible, and his place was behind the driver, a Texas Department of Public Safety officer. Stoughton positioned himself for a better view, not in the seat, but on top of the boot which contained the folded convertible top. To his right was Art Rickerby, staff photographer for *LIFE* magazine, with Henry Burroughs of Associated Press next to Rickerby. Frank Cancellare, veteran United Press International photographer was on the right, virtually straddling the front and back seats. *Dallas Morning News* photographer Clint Grant, who had accompanied the presidential trip from its beginning in Washington, had been invited to ride in the front seat next to the driver. The photographers' silver 1964 Chevrolet Impala was the seventh behind the President's car, it now being behind the motion picture car, the positions exchanged from the earlier Fort Worth motorcade.[33]

Conversation in Stoughton's car centered on the size of the crowd, waiting for some action in the President's car, and anticipation of the luncheon speech at the Trade Mart. The crowds began to grow and then to swell with people eight or more deep on the sidewalks as the motorcade traveled through the downtown area.

Stoughton shoots a view of the Dallas motorcade as it travels down Main Street toward intersecting Griffin Street. In the distant background trees indicate the beginning of a park area known as Dealey Plaza.

Having used up half of his film magazine at the airport, Stoughton shot only one picture during the motorcade. He figured to save the remainder of his roll for events at the Trade Mart. The picture he made was taken from his position on the back left of the Impala looking straight down Main Street. In the foreground and slightly out of focus are the occupants of the motion picture camera car, including the crew-cut head of CBS's Tom Craven. A hatted Dave Wiegman is apparently in the process of taking movies of the crowd, while a leaning Tom Atkins is just behind Wiegman. To their front is seen the blue telephone car occupied by the wire service representatives, then Mayor Cabell's car and in front of that the sedan VP follow-up car with a door on the driver's side ajar so that if there was any trouble the agents could quickly exit. In front of this car, but out of view save for seeing Lady Bird Johnson's head looking backwards as seen through the window of the follow-up car, is the Vice-President's vehicle. Agents on the side running-board of the President's follow-up car are visible in shadow as are police motorcycles flanking the Lincoln. Neither the presidential car nor its occupants are discernible. Further down Main Street four of the lead motorcycle policemen are glimpsed, and in the extreme background appear trees which delineate an open area unfamiliar to Stoughton, and known locally as Dealey Plaza.

This photograph reveals that Stoughton's car is approaching a cross-street marked "Griffin," and on both sides of the street are large crowds. Red, white, and blue bunting is draped on wires across the street and a clock on a building sign indicates the time as 12:22. The commercial buildings in evidence are unremarkable and include the Hotel Maurice, upon which a painted wall ad indicates it is "fireproof" and available for rates of "$1 up per day." On the opposite side of the street from the hotel a gold star tops the neon sign for the Texas Bank, while still further down Main Street one may spy the conical towers of the old County Court House located on the corner of Main and Houston Streets. The sky is cloudless, and the effects of a breeze are evident in the fluttering of the parade bunting. In only a few minutes the motorcade will turn right onto Houston Street and into history.[34]

Just after Stoughton's car had made its turn at the old Court House, he heard three very distinct, loud reports which sounded like shots. "I remember at the time when I heard the shots I was sitting on the outside of the car and Art was sitting next to me. I said 'Hey, Art, these Texans really know how to welcome a guy, don't they?' In my mind I saw a guy on the roof in a ten-gallon hat with a six-shooter – bang bang! bang bang! That's what I thought. Then we rounded the corner and saw nothing except a lot of hectic police activity. So then the jollity went out of the statement and it seemed like serious business."[35]

After traveling the short distance on Houston Street and making a sharp left onto Elm Street and past the red brick Texas School Book Depository building, Stoughton recalls, "We realized something was amiss, as the cars ahead of us were gone. As we rolled to a stop just around the corner, Cancellare leaped out of the car and ran to take a picture of a family cowering on the grass. Tom Atkins was already there shooting his 16mm Ariflex, and instead of doing likewise, I slipped on my 150mm lens on the Hasselblad and shot one frame. . . ."[36]

The most obvious focal point in the confusion of the moment was toward the four members of the Newman family. Mr. and Mrs. Bill Newman and their two young sons had been watching the procession. When the shots sounded, the father yelled for the family to "Hit the ground!" Most of the press people at the scene momentarily gravitated their attention to the dramatic action of bodies falling.

In the Stoughton photograph three of the Newmans are visible on the ground, with Mrs. Gail Newman looking toward the street and obscuring her four-year-old son Billy from Stoughton's lens. Bill Newman

Shortly after shots were fired at the motorcade, Stoughton takes a picture of the activity at the scene. The Newman family lie on the ground as cameramen Tom Craven and Tom Atkins film their distress. In the background is the soon-to-be infamous "Grassy Knoll," including the concrete retaining wall and stockade fence. Some witnesses and many subsequent researchers believed one or more assassins possibly fired from a location in this general area.

This frame of film taken by cameraman Jimmy Darnell of WBAP-TV after he had jumped out of Camera Car 3, shows Camera Cars 1 and 2 cruising down Elm Street following the shooting. Stoughton is on the left rear side of the second vehicle preparing to take a picture of the scene on the knoll to his right.

clasps two-year-old Clayton, while gazing toward the photographers. Hovering over them in an unnatural pose is Tom Craven finishing up taking film of the couple. He had followed Wiegman, now out of view, to this spot. Tom Atkins is behind and to the right of Craven's position, looking through the viewfinder of his Ariflex movie camera. To his rear can be seen the crouching figure of a woman wearing sunglasses. The original negative of this picture is marked "8" in sequence, and is the last taken in color by Stoughton in Dallas. A full, uncropped view of this print reveals on the extreme left side of the negative and almost obscured by a lamp-post shaft on Elm Street, two persons sitting on the concrete steps leading to the wall on the knoll above the street. These

Dallas Morning News *photographer Tom Dillard, who had also jumped out of Camera Car 3, takes this quick shot of the three camera cars on Elm Street following the assassination. This view looking toward the Dealey Plaza triple underpass includes Stoughton's camera car in front of the other two, it having driven around the first car which stopped to pick up the several cameramen. Spectator James Tague, seen in the extreme left background at the under-pass base, was struck in the cheek by a chip of curbstone which had been possibly fragmented by an assassin's bullet.*

are two of the three men who had been standing near the steps at the time of the assassination. The stockade fence separating the railroad parking area from the Plaza, and a portion of the concrete peristyle and the pedestal from which spectator and amateur movie-maker Abraham Zapruder had moments ago filmed the shooting, are visible in the upper half of the photograph.[37]

After making this quick picture of what would later become refered to as the "Grassy Knoll," Stoughton had no time to take others of the area. As soon as he realized something had happened and that the President's car was gone, he "wanted to get out of there – get to where it was going," even if that meant having to leave UPI photographer Cancellare behind. Stoughton nonetheless wanted to be where the President was. He yelled to the driver, "Let's get the hell out of here!" Leaving the scene Stoughton observed an abandoned police motorcycle, while a cop with pistol in hand was running up the knoll embankment.[38]

The car, now with only four photographers aboard, drove directly to the Trade Mart, its occupants only knowing that something highly unusual had occurred back at the Plaza. Stoughton recollects people yelling towards the car as it drove through the Trade Mart that "He's at Parkland!" This meant nothing to Stoughton, but to Clint Grant, the local photographer on board, it was an obvious reference. Grant commanded, "God, that's a hospital! Let's take off!" With that the driver rushed the photographers to Parkland Memorial Hospital.[39]

Stoughton's car arrived near Parkland's emergency entrance at about the same time as the other two camera cars. Grabbing his 35mm Alpa Reflex camera loaded with a fresh roll of Tri-X film, Stoughton made two quick shots of the emergency entrance. Assistant Press Secretary Kilduff, cigarette in mouth, is there, as is film-maker Wiegman. Stoughton's boss, General Clifton is in one frame, while Dallas motorcycle cops and plainclothes officers have formed a rough cordon around the three-bay "Ambulance Only" entrance. A number of civilians, including many hospital personnel, mill around the area, and the presidential limousine is head-first in the middle bay, flanked by two parked ambulances.

A bit later Stoughton made two more pictures of the area, but taken from a different angle, showing agents putting the plastic bubble-top and fabric cover on over the convertible. The trunk is open and a metal bucket is on the ground next to the President's door. Stoughton recalls that a man was washing the seat "with a cloth, and he had a bucket. There was blood all over the seat, and flower petals and stuff on the floor."[40]

Stoughton then went into the hospital. By this time he had learned that the President was seriously wounded by an assassination attempt. He remembers that at the appearance of a priest on the scene General Clifton glanced at Stoughton and both men's eyes filled up.[41]

Stoughton would have missed the opportunity to take the most important photographs of his career, had he not happened to be in the hospital at the right moment. Signal Corpsman Art Bales was attempting to supply communications to the outside world from Parkland Hospital, and according to Stoughton, "He handed me a phone at a critical time when he had just touched base with the White House switchboard in Washington. He had an open line, and had to go do something else and asked me to hold this phone and talk into it so that the operator would not listen in, find nobody there, and cut them off. So just as he handed me the receiver I saw Johnson and Lady Bird going out the 'Out' door rather quickly and I said, 'Where's he going?' and when [Bales] said, 'The President is going to Washington,' I knew that President Kennedy had expired and I said, 'So am I,' and handed him back his phone."[42]

Stoughton believed it his duty to be with the new President, but he was not quick enough to catch a ride with the small, fast-departing entourage. Just after Johnson

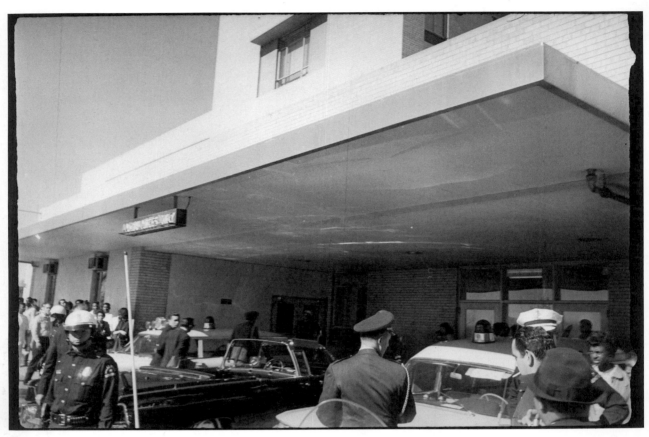

Stoughton arrives to find the President's car parked head first in the Parkland Hospital ambulance bay.

In the midst of the hospital confusion, cameraman Dave Wiegman films Press Secretary Kilduff approaching him.

A bucket at his feet, an agent is seen leaning into the back seat of the Lincoln cleaning up some of the gore.

Roof panels and fabric covering have been removed from the trunk and attached to the top of the vehicle.

At 2:05 p.m. CST, while Stoughton was already at Love Field, President Kennedy's body was removed from Parkland Hospital to transport it to Air Force One. *This* Dallas Morning News *photo shows Mrs. Kennedy entering the ambulance-hearse, preparing to leave the hospital.*

left the hospital at 1:26 p.m., however, vice-presidential Secret Service Agent Thomas L. Johns arrived, also having missed the departure. Johns obtained a police car and driver, and with Stoughton and Johnson aides Cliff Carter and Jack Valenti, they made for Love Field.[43]

Stoughton remembers the ride as "hairy and fast." The driver did not know how to get to the plane, and found himself on the opposite side of the tarmac. Normally in such a situation, the occupants would have laboriously threaded their way around to the other side, but the day was far from normal. Johns, who had earlier that day been left on Elm Street by his follow-up car when he had jumped from the car upon the first inkling of trouble in order to run to the Johnson car, did not want to be left behind again. He shouted to the car's occupants that they were on the opposite side and "Let's shoot the runways."[44] Contrary to airport rules, common sense,

and security dictates, they managed to reach their destination without being run over or shot.

President Johnson had decided to travel back to Washington on board *Air Force One* with its more sophisticated communications system, rather than on *Air Force Two*. He did not want to depart, however, until he had taken the oath of office and the deceased President and his widow were also aboard. Back at Parkland, Assistant Press Secretary Kilduff made the public announcement of the death of President Kennedy at 1:30 p.m. Central Standard Time. Dallas undertaker Vernon O'Neal was notified to bring over a casket, and he arrived with a 400-pound bronze Elgin Brittania model in which the wrapped President's body was placed. Following an ugly confrontation between members of the entourage and Medical Examiner Dr. Earl Rose over removal of the body from the Dallas jurisdiction, at about 2:05 the casket left the hospital in an O'Neal ambulance-hearse.

Stoughton had not taken any photographs of the confused and devastated staff inside Parkland's corridors due to his own shock. Aboard *Air Force One*, however, he observed the ambulance arriving, and from the forward port-side hatch of the Boeing 707 he made a series of 11 shots with his 35mm Alpa, finishing off the black-and-white roll he had begun at Parkland's emergency entrance.

The series begins at about 2:14 with the ambulance arriving near the rear gangway to *Air Force One*. Driven by SA Andy Berger, Agent Stewart G. Stout, Jr., is in the middle front seat and Assistant Agent-in-Charge Roy Kellerman on the passenger side. Hidden from view are Mrs.

Kennedy, presidential physician Dr. George Burkley, and SA Clint Hill, riding in the rear of the ambulance with the coffin. Behind the ambulance follows a light colored sedan with aides Larry O'Brien, Dave Powers, and Ken O'Donnell keeping close by their fallen chief. Two uniformed airmen are at the bottom of the gangway, while in the background three Dallas policemen are among those providing security for the plane.

In the second photograph Stoughton has panned slightly to the right. Several other vehicles are seen, including a Mercury Comet convertible with its top closed and marked with a number "1" on the windshield. Less than two hours ago this was the vehicle carrying Mayor Cabell and his wife in the motorcade.

This full-frame image, including sprocket holes and frame number, is the sixth picture taken by Stoughton in the sequence of President Kennedy's casket being taken aboard Air Force One.

More uniformed police are in view, as is Dallas Police Chief Jesse Curry in civilian clothes. Curry had earlier driven President Johnson from Parkland to the airplane. Also seen are various Secret Service agents and members of President Kennedy's staff, including his secretary, Evelyn Lincoln. In the next six photographs, Stoughton captures the carrying of the casket up the gangway, as agents struggle with the almost 600-pound load on the narrow metal stairs. Numerous hands attempt to help with the burden, while on the tarmac below Military Aides Clifton and Godfrey McHugh, Mrs. Kennedy, and members of the President's loyal "Irish Mafia" watch with what looks to be expressions of shock and confusion. A uniformed Dallas police officer a few paces behind the melancholy gathering is seen in three subsequent frames. He removes his hat and, in a poignant and private salute, holds it to his heart until the casket is aboard. The final three frames in the sequence follow the former First Lady walking up the steps looking forlorn and disheveled with blood spatters on her skirt and stocking. Behind trudge O'Brien and O'Donnell, followed by Powers, whose downcast look reflects more than simply watching his foothold.

This sad sequence, more than any written description, conveys the feelings of confusion and haphazardness following the events of the last hours. It depicts an obscene twist of fate when compared to the jaunty, bright, elegant and stately arrival of the President and his wife down this same gangway an era ago.[45]

Stoughton reloaded his Alpa with Tri-X 400 ASA film and put in a roll of 120 black-and-white film in his Hasselblad, as he wanted fast film if he were called upon to make pictures of the swearing-in. Kilduff confirmed to him that the President wanted to record the ceremony, and about 15 minutes after President Kennedy's body was aboard, Federal Judge Sarah T. Hughes arrived to administer the oath. Stoughton suggested to Kilduff that they use the airplane Dictaphone to record the

swearing-in, thus creating both a photographic and audio record of the event.[46]

The oath-taking ceremony would take place in the stateroom, which had the largest open space in the cabin. It was unencumbered by seating, save for two built-in tables, a sofa, and chair. The approximately 16-foot square space, however, was still much too small to accommodate everyone on the plane. Looking over the area, Stoughton stepped up on the sofa and had to "flatten himself against the rear bulkhead of the compartment," in order to get the best view of the proceedings.[47]

Dean UPI White House reporter Merriman Smith, who had been in Georgia 18 years earlier to file stories on the death of Franklin D. Roosevelt, wrote concerning this scene he was now witnessing, "The compartment became hotter and hotter. Johnson was worried that some of the Kennedy staff might not be able to get inside. He urged people to press forward, but a signal corps photographer, Capt. Cecil Stoughton, standing in the corner on a chair, said if Johnson moved any closer, it would be virtually impossible to make a truly historic photograph."[48]

Stoughton's physical position was uncomfortable enough, and in the ever stuffier compartment, his body felt sticky and clammy. He also felt the professional pressure of not muffing this assignment, the most important of his career. Johnson asked Stoughton how he wanted them, and the photographer replied that he would place Judge Hughes so that the camera view would be over her shoulder. Upon learning that Mrs. Kennedy would be present, he suggested that she should be on one side of the President with Mrs. Johnson on the other.[49]

Stoughton began his picture series at about 2:33 p.m. using his Alpa and shooting with available cabin light. The first six pictures show Johnson as the focal point of the camera's lens with others awkwardly waiting. Among those seen in these first pictures are Judge Hughes, Lady Bird Johnson, Congressmen Jack Brooks, Albert Thomas and Homer Thornberry.

The second photograph taken in Cecil Stoughton's black and white Hasselblad series shows President Johnson and others in the stateroom awaiting the arrival of Mrs. Kennedy.

Enlargements of 12 of the 13 contact prints of Stoughton's 35mm swearing-in series made from the negatives now preserved at the Lyndon B. Johnson Presidential Library. "The wink" negative, the next to last in the series, is not present among those at the Johnson Library.

Also noted among the spectators in the Stoughton sequence are General Clifton, Larry O'Brien, Ken O'Donnell, *Newsweek* correspondent Charles Roberts, Police Chief Jesse Curry, Press Secretary Kilduff, Johnson aides Bill Moyers and Jack Valenti, Pilot Jim Swindal, Agents Jerry Kivett, and Lem Johns, Evelyn Lincoln, Mary Gallagher, and Pam Turnure.[50]

Switching to his Hasselblad camera, Stoughton began to take another photo with his favorite camera equipped with a flash unit. For a moment he felt a sinking sensation through his body. As he recalls, "The first time I pushed the button, it didn't work and I about died. I had a little connector that was just loose because of all the bustling around, and I just pushed it with my finger and number two went off on schedule. I sprayed the cabin so I could get a picture of everybody there." Prints of the first two Hasselblad photos Stoughton made cover a larger area than the 35mm prints and are much crisper in detail. Unlike the 35mm prints taken with available light, these flash shots fill in the scene with light and show mirror reflections from the overhead lighting rather than white light. Judge Hughes can be seen holding a Roman Catholic missal, believed at the time to be a Bible, for the swearing-in ceremony, together with a sheet of paper imprinted with the presidential seal and the words "Aboard Air Force One." Typed on the sheet of paper is the presidential oath-of-office beginning with the words "I do solemnly swear (or affirm)."[51]

Everyone was awaiting the arrival of Mrs. Kennedy, who moments after the eighth Stoughton picture is taken, enters the room with Ken O'Donnell. Following a few remarks of sympathy awkwardly, but sincerely expressed by some present, the former First Lady moves, with O'Donnell and Powers nearby, to the President's left side. Stoughton had already seen the sickening blood stains on Mrs. Kennedy's dress, and knew that photographing them in these soon-to-be-famous pictures would be terribly inappropriate. He made sure the lens would not reveal the stains.

It was now very cramped quarters. Merriman Smith, Dave Powers, Dr. George Burkley, Johnson secretary Liz Carpenter, and Agents Henry Rybka and Roy Kellerman are now also in partial view of Stoughton's camera lens. Judge Hughes is given the nod to begin the oath. It is 2:38 p.m. CST and Kilduff holds up the microphone and depresses the button while Stoughton quickly clicks off four shots with the Hasselblad and four with the Alpa. Except for the words of the oath, everyone was quiet, and Stoughton realized that the only other sound in the cabin was the clicking of the shutter and the clanking of his equipment.

All faces are somber. The hulking form of President Lyndon Johnson is surrounded by a triangle of three women. His large right hand is raised and held seemingly uncomfortably tight to his body. Johnson rests his left palm on the missal, Judge Hughes's thumb in contact with his hand. Lady Bird, as ever, stands next to her husband. Her sad eyes stare towards the judge whose words are confirming a new and heavy burden upon her husband and family. The body of Jacqueline Kennedy is present, giving a manifestation of continuity and grace, yet her soul and mind are elsewhere in a personal hell.[52]

The ceremony was over within half a minute. Congratulations mixed with expressions of sympathy were exchanged by many, and Stoughton finished off his take with five pictures as Johnson turns away.

Two original negatives from the Stoughton take of the swearing-in are not preserved within the Lyndon Baines Johnson Library collection. One is a Hasselblad of the swearing-in itself, while the other, a 35mm shot, captures the cabin following the ceremony. These pictures, though not present as original negatives, are available at the Johnson Library in a cropped print format. The 35mm negative may have been excluded from those given over to the Johnson Library due to what someone may have construed as its picturing what the public might perceive as a seemingly

One of eight frames made during the taking of the oath of office, this one is the first of the four Hasselblad swearing-in images.

The last of the 35mm swearing-in photos. Ken O'Donnell stands at Mrs. Kennedy's left side.

A full-frame image of "the wink" photo, published here in its entirety for the first time.

inappropriate gesture. President Johnson is looking toward his friend Congressman Albert Thomas. Though Thomas might just be caught in a mid-blink, the picture conveys the sense that he is captured on film in the middle of winking at Johnson.

A number of conspiracy theorists have found this picture to be more than a simply inelegant yet private gesture, but rather evidence captured fortuitously on film of a conspiratorial acknowledgment of some kind on the part of the new President and a Texas congressman. Sometimes, however, a wink is just a wink. It can just as easily be interpreted as Thomas making a fleeting contact with the new President in a gesture of good luck, or perhaps as a sign of empathy. Sometimes we can make more of a gesture or facial contortion captured on film in a fragment of time than is warranted. Such conception is one of the pitfalls of photographic interpretation. This author suspects, but cannot prove, that someone saw in this negative what they thought might be construed by others as an inappropriate gesture given the morbid nature of the circumstances surrounding the swearing-in, and an attempt was made to get rid of the negative.

Commenting upon this photo, Cecil Stoughton confesses to being disturbed by the potential consequences which publishing it might bring. He points out that, "We, of course, will never know for sure, and it would seem to me, at this time, that to infer sinister thoughts in the mind of Mr. Thomas would be taking an extreme liberty which could not be debated by him, or others." When asked his view of what it all meant, Stoughton couched his serious thoughts in a bit of his typical humor. "Let it be said that I have always taken the darker road in describing how I feel about it – that is to say, I see an enigmatic expression which could be innocent, or sinister, and I have leaned to the latter – but then, I am a rather negative person (hence my interest in photography – Ha)." Stoughton's full series of photographs inside the stateroom included 13 frames of 35mm and 8 of 120 film.[53]

Following the oath-taking ceremony, Johnson ordered *Air Force One* to Washington. Those who were to remain in Dallas quickly scurried off the plane. Stoughton was among those staying behind. He would have his unprocessed film developed and sent out via the wire services as a reassurance that the government continued. Kilduff handed Stoughton the dictabelt recording of the oath-of-office, and never before had the captain been singularly more responsible for history's remembrance of a momentous event.

Here was the photographer who, through his camera work at the 1961 Kennedy inauguration had been brought to the attention of the President and had obtained the position of White House Photographer. That earlier inauguration had been full of ceremony, positive expectation, and chilling cold weather. Now Stoughton was there at the end of the cycle, or rather the beginning of a new one. Absent was all that makes inaugurations special, save for the transfer of power. The oath was the same, but joy and pomp had been replaced with sorrow and uncertainty, and the ceremony was conducted in a stuffy, tube-like space. Yet the visible continuity of the republic, no matter how erratically it had been carried out, had in fact been accomplished. The government continued. And Stoughton was carrying the proof.

No one was allowed to enter or leave the air strip until *Air Force One* took off, and just about the time the plane became airborne at 2:48 p.m., a press bus from Parkland Hospital arrived on the scene. Pool reporter Sid Davis, who had been aboard during the swearing-in, recounted the events to the other reporters who quickly gathered around him. Stoughton was met by his car companions Cancellare and Burroughs, veteran cameramen whom Stoughton greatly respected.

What to do about the undeveloped pictures? A nickel was flipped to see which bureau would accommodate developing of these historic pictures, and Burroughs's Associated Press office won the toss. The three dashed down to the Dallas Morning News building, where the AP bureau was located, and the film was given over to AP photographer/technician Robert A. Jarboe. Stoughton "went into the darkroom with him, even though there was nothing I could do. I just wanted to be there when it came out. And when he held it up to the light, I could see some images and then I breathed. I was turning blue up to that point."[54]

One of the four Hasselblad prints of the oath-taking was chosen as the picture to send over the wire, and through mutual agreement the picture would not be sent out on the AP drum until a duplicate copy was delivered to United Press International for simultaneous distribution. In their caption material sent along with the photograph, both wire services gave Captain Cecil Stoughton photo credit, and soon his photograph was reproduced around the world in newspapers under headlines such as "Lyndon Johnson takes helm after Kennedy assassinated." Even before being reproduced in newspapers, wirephoto copies of the picture were flashed on network television, NBC telecasting it at about 5:40 p.m. Eastern Standard Time.[55]

Later that day Stoughton received a phone call from Kenny O'Donnell, who had been reading Merriman Smith's wire story concerning the swearing-in of Johnson. Stoughton remembers, "O'Donnell was reading the stories about Jackie being covered in blood, and me taking pictures all in the same breath. He visualized that I was taking pictures of her covered with blood. So he got in touch with me at the laboratory there at the AP office, and said what the hell do I mean putting out pictures like that? I said, 'Kenny, you haven't seen the pictures.' So he said, 'You get your ass back here.'" Stoughton, Cancellare and Burroughs hitched a ride back to Washington on an Air Force Jet Star that evening. Upon arriving in Washington, Stoughton went to his lab and had 8" x 10" prints made of all the swearing-in negatives, none of them showing any blood stains on Mrs. Kennedy's clothing. According to Stoughton, O'Donnell was being very protective of Mrs. Kennedy, and even though her stained clothes and stocking were very evident at the landing of *Air Force One* back at Andrews Air Force Base around 6:05 p.m., he did not want the swearing-in pictures to show such a scene, and had been reading into what the pictures showed without seeing the pictures themselves.[56]

Faith Stoughton, the mother of Cecil's three children, worked at the Pentagon, and when the first bulletin of the Dallas shooting was heard on Friday afternoon, Mrs. Stoughton was very upset and concerned. She had envisioned her husband on the back step of the car, where on numerous occasions he had found a perch on such motorcades. She feared he might have been shot himself. Such speculation was not helped when a spurious report circulated for a time that an agent had also been shot at the scene. Faith breathed easier once her husband had spoken to her and was back in Washington.

The photographer was not ready to go home, however, and following his visit to the lab he went to the White House. He was there to record the body being escorted back into the Executive Mansion in the early morning of November 23. The next few days blur in Stoughton's memory. "I was going all day Friday, Friday night, and shooting pictures at 4 o'clock in the morning. I went back home, changed clothes, and went back to the White House for the visits of all the dignitaries to Johnson and all his meetings. Then the lying in state in the East Room and the Capitol and the funeral. And when we got to St. Matthew's on Monday, I was up on the steps as they were carrying the casket, and I could reach out and touch the flag, and I just collapsed at that point. But I carried on, went to the cemetery and shot everything there that I could. But I must have been going just on nerves."[57]

Tom Atkins also recorded the Washington funeral events. As the cortege was leaving the White House for Capitol Hill on Sunday, ". . . the car with Mrs. Kennedy and little John-John came by. And he was up over the back of the seat

Captain Stoughton is there at the White House at 4:34 a.m., Saturday, November 23, to record the arrival of the President's casket through the mansion's front entrance. The military honor guard moves through the White House Entrance Hall toward the East Room, followed by Mrs. Kennedy, who is escorted by her brother-in-law, Attorney General Robert F. Kennedy.

On Monday, November 25, Stoughton records the final chapter as the President's casket is carried into St. Matthew's Cathedral in Washington, D.C.

and he had this strange look. I saw that and I sat down on the north lawn of the White House and just bawled my eyes out." On Monday, while photographing at the funeral, Atkins recalled, "They were going into the church and I saw Cecil Stoughton in my viewfinder. And I saw him just sit down and start to bawl. We've never talked about it."[58]

Following that long weekend Stoughton had expected to be interviewed by investigators concerning the assassination, but was not contacted. Concerning himself and other press photographers, he commented, "They think of us being there, and yet we're not there."

Stoughton remained on as White House photographer and felt his relationship with President Johnson was quite good. As he recalls concerning Johnson, "He liked pictures and I had something he wanted – a camera." In half-jest Stoughton remembers that he and the White House physician were the two most popular people with Johnson, and that his access to the President was much less restricted than under Kennedy. He remained at the White House past the 1964 election and into 1965. In the spring of 1965 Mrs. Kennedy requested Stoughton to accompany her and family and friends as they participated in a ceremony at Runnymede, England, on May 14, 1965, dedicating a parcel of land to the memory of the fallen President. Speaking personally to President Johnson, Stoughton asked permission to make the trip, and he was told it was OK for him to go. A week following his return, Stoughton abruptly received orders transferring him out of the White House. Thus ended his assignment as White House photographer. Stoughton worked out of a Pentagon office until his retirement from the Army in April 1967, to become chief photographer for the National Park Service, retiring from his long government service in April 1973.[59]

Biographer William Manchester interviewed Stoughton and scores of others for his 1967 book *Death of a President*; and while Stoughton feels that most of Manchester's facts were correct, he does believe that Manchester embellished the conflicting mood and confrontational air aboard *Air Force One* during the time of the swearing-in ceremony. Manchester noted in his book and in subsequent interviews that most every Kennedy aide had insultingly circumvented the oath-taking. In February 1967 the *Boston Globe* published one of Stoughton's pictures depicting Kenny O'Donnell next to Mrs. Kennedy together with a story refuting the charge. A follow-up story about Stoughton and including reproductions of 19 of his pictures was published by *TIME* magazine two weeks later.[60]

On occasion Stoughton was approached by other assassination researchers, including David S. Lifton, who published a highly successful book, *Best Evidence*, in 1980 in which he claimed a conspiracy involving a possible casket switch and alteration of evidence on the President's body. Lifton used nine of Stoughton's pictures and spoke to the photographer. Stoughton later succinctly commented, "The Lifton theory is ridiculous. You can rule him out." Though Stoughton admits to having read extensively about the assassination, he does not have any strong feelings about a conspiracy, save to say that it is hard to believe that one man could have done it. If there was a conspiracy, he hopes somebody got burned on it. None of the theories he has read, however, seems to have great merit.[61]

The cameras Stoughton used for his historic recording of the events of November 22, 1963, were Army property and later returned to the Pentagon. Stoughton was told they were later sold as surplus property.[62]

Decades after the events of November 1963, a tanned and relaxed Cecil and Faith Stoughton live in retirement near Cocoa Beach, Florida. In 1973, along with Ted Clifton and *TIME* reporter Hugh Sidey, he co-authored a book of photographs and reminiscences titled, *The Memories: JFK, 1961-1963*. Stoughton's book dedication reflects the feelings he had for his unique job. "The 1,065 days of the presidency of John F. Kennedy were my golden days, filled with the special joy of living and working with young and vital people who had found a cause beyond themselves. Those days were not without personal sacrifices, prolonged periods of absence from my family were necessary. My wife Faith and children Bill, Jamie, and Sharon carried on cheerfully and gracefully, even though they could not share in my special experience. . . ."[63]

Concerning his anonymous contribution in recording presidential history on film, Stoughton, who has been described by friends as good natured, self-effacing, and loyal, comments simply, "The President knew I took them. I know I took them and my wife knows I took them. I guess that's enough credit."[64]

CHAPTER NOTES

1. Cecil Stoughton, *The Memories: JFK, 1961-1963*, p. 199.
2. Letter, Stoughton to Trask, 5/6/1985.
3. *Memories*, op. cit., p. 199; Telephone interview of Stoughton, 7/10/1985.
4. Stoughton interview on ABC's *Good Morning America*, 11/22/1983.
5. Telephone interview of Stoughton, 7/10/1985.
6. *Memories*, op. cit., p. 137.
7. Ibid.; John G. Morris, "Shooting the Presidents," *Popular Photography*, 8/1977, p. 80-81; Telephone interview of Thomas M. Atkins, 3/19/1986.
8. Telephone interview, 7/10/1985.
9. *Memories*, op. cit., p. 153.
10. Telephone interview, 7/10/1985.
11. Ibid.
12. Ibid.
13. Ibid.; *Memories*, op. cit., p. 153-155.
14. Telephone interview, 7/10/1985; Letter, Stoughton to Trask, 5/6/1985.
15. Telephone interview, 7/10/1985.
16. Ibid.
17. Letter, Allan B. Goodrich to Trask, 4/15/1985.
18. Ibid.
19. Telephone interview, 7/10/1985.
20. Ibid.
21. *Good Morning America*, op. cit.
22. *Report of the House Select Committee on Assassinations*, p. 35-36.
23. William Manchester, *Death of a President*, p. 62-63.
24. Stoughton White House photo sequence, 525, #4-20.
25. Stoughton White House photo sequence, C420, #36-38, 33; *Year: Encyclopedia News Annual*, 1963, p. [9].
26. Stoughton White House photo sequence, C420, #31, 34, 32, 46, 45, 48, 47.
27. Ibid., C420, #49, 50.
28. Telephone interview, 7/10/1985.
29. Ibid.; *Good Morning America*, op. cit.
30. Stoughton White House photo sequence, C420, #51, 15, 16, 13-14.
31. Ibid., C420, #19, 20, 17. This Hasselblad 120 negative filmstrip was marked with a red serial number: 8 06018. The three-minute Powers color film of the Texas trip is now preserved at the Kennedy Library.
32. Ibid., C420, #18, 23, 24; Telephone interview, 7/10/1985.
33. Letter, Stoughton to Trask, 5/6/1985.
34. Stoughton White House photo sequence, C420, #21. The last film clip made by presidential aide Dave Powers from his position in the Secret Service follow-up car just behind the President's car is also of the scene on Main Street at the Griffin cross street. It shows SA Clint Hill riding on the rear of the President's car.
35. Telephone interview, 7/10/1985.
36. Letter, Stoughton to Trask, 5/6/1985.
37. Stoughton White House photo sequence, C420, #22.
38. Letter, Stoughton to Trask, 5/6/1985; Telephone interview, 7/10/1985.
39. Telephone interview, 7/10/1985.
40. Telephone interview, 7/10/1985; Stoughton Parkland-AF1 photo sequence #2-5.
41. Manchester, op. cit., p. 215.
42. Telephone interview, 7/10/1985.
43. Memorandum, To chief: U. S. Secret Service, From: ASAIC Thomas L. Johns, 11/29/1963, p. 2-3.
44. Manchester, op. cit., p. 239.
45. Stoughton Parkland-AF1 photo sequence, #6-16.
46. John B. Mayo, *Bulletin From Dallas*, p. 118.
47. Charles Roberts, *The Truth About the Assassination*, p. 113; Interview of Stoughton, 4/23/1986.
48. Merriman Smith, *The Murder of the Young President*, p. [5]; Rufus W. Youngblood, *Twenty Years With the Secret Service*, p. 130.
49. Manchester, op. cit., p. 322.
50. Stoughton Tri-X film aboard AF1, photo sequence #0-5.
51. Telephone interview, 7/10/1985; Interview, 4/23/1986; Stoughton 120 film aboard AF1, photo sequence #2-3.
52. Stoughton Tri-X film, op. cit., photo sequence #6-9 and 120 film, photo sequence #4-7.
53. Letter, Stoughton to Trask, 1/23/1997. The "wink" photo was the twelfth in the 35mm sequence, while the missing Hasselblad 120 negative was the sixth in that roll sequence.
54. Telephone interview, 7/10/1985.
55. *The Clarion-Ledger* [Jackson, Mississippi], 11/22/1963, p. 1.; *There Was a President*, p. 31. Also sent out was a copy of Stoughton's Tri-X #10 print which showed the President and Mrs. Johnson speaking to Mrs. Kennedy shortly after the oath. In the AP wirephoto caption it mentions, "Picture was made by Capt. Cecil Stoughton, official White House photographer, who was the lone cameraman allowed at the scene." (*Fort Worth Star-Telegram*, 11/23/1963, p.1)
56. Telephone interview, 7/10/1985.
57. Ibid.
58. Telephone interview of Atkins, 3/19/1986.
59. Telephone interview of Stoughton, 7/10/1985.; *TIME*, 2/24/1967, p. 19; Letter Stoughton to Trask, 12/28/1996.
60. *New York Times*, 2/10/1967, p. 15; *TIME*, 2/24/1967, p. 20-21.
61. Telephone interview, 7/10/1985; Letter, Stoughton to Trask, 6/3/1985.
62. Letter, Stoughton to Trask, 5/6/1985.
63. *Memories*, op. cit., dedication.
64. Interview, 4/23/1986.

CHAPTER 2

The AP Man

Numerous photographers were on hand to record the last moments in the life of the thirty-fifth President of the United States. Most of these picture-takers around Dealey Plaza were non-professionals who had simply wanted to capture on film a fleeting glimpse or two of the infrequent visit of an American President to their state and city. If the event had turned out to be just a typical motorcade, these amateur pictures would soon have been relegated to the near obscurity of the family photo album or stored in a slide box tucked away into a bureau drawer or on a bookshelf.

A number of White House, national, and local press photographers were traveling in the motorcade from Love Air Field to the Dallas Trade Mart in vehicles many car-lengths away from the presidential Lincoln. These professionals would occasionally take a few feet of movie film or a photo of the large downtown crowd with the VIP vehicles barely visible up ahead. Yet of the scores of people, both amateur and professional, who would take pictures of the events before, during, and after the few seconds of shots that would sidetrack the course of American history, no other photographer was at the scene with more premeditated camera planning than Jim Altgens, a man not originally even scheduled to be viewing the parade.

~

James William Altgens, known as "Ike," to his friends and co-workers, was, except for his service during World War II, a life-long resident of Dallas, having been born there on April 28, 1919. Orphaned as a child, Altgens was reared by a widowed aunt. In 1938, at the age of nineteen, he began his long career with Associated Press. Associated Press and United Press International were the two competitive,

New York based, national news-gathering organizations which electronically sent information out to newspaper, government, radio, television and other subscribers throughout the world.

James W. Altgens in 1963

Altgens initially worked at odd jobs in the local Dallas AP bureau, including keeping track of payments for part-time reporters known as "stringers," and doing occasional sports writing. In February 1940 he began to work within the wirephoto department. Following his return to Dallas from Coast Guard service, and his marriage to Clara B. Halliburton in July 1944, Altgens, in 1945, began taking photographs for the Associated Press News Bureau. A graduate of North Dallas High School, Altgens, while working for AP, attended Southern Methodist University night school. He completed his academic work after six years and earned a Bachelor of Arts degree in speech with a journalism minor. During those early years Altgens was often sent out of town on assignments and would have to bring his books with him so he could study when he had a chance. "I just kept plugging, and got through it and got my degree."[1]

By the 1960s, Altgens, a genial Texan with large facial features, a low melodic voice, and a receding hairline with a rake of white hair on top, was serving the Dallas bureau of the Associated Press as a wirephoto operator, though often functioning as a photographer, and sometimes filling in as news photo editor.

Altgens also enjoyed occasional work acting in television commercials and doing modeling for magazine and newspaper advertisements. In 1959 Altgens played the role of a U.S. Secretary of Defense in a science fiction movie titled, "Beyond the Time Barrier." Directed by Edgar Giulmer, the 75-minute black & white film shot in Texas, told the story of a test pilot who punched his vehicle into the future to find society overcome by plague. Altgens had the final line in the movie – "That's a lot to think about!" – which line he got a kick out of recalling.

Residing with his wife Clara about two miles north of University Park, Altgens covered numerous local events, including sports photography of AFL and Bowl games. He had photographed John F. Kennedy once before. In November 1961 the new President, accompanied by former President Dwight D. Eisenhower, arrived at Perrin Air Force Base to attend the funeral of Speaker of the House of Representatives Sam Rayburn, in Bonham, Texas. Just prior to this assignment, Altgens had climbed to the twenty-ninth floor of the Dallas Mercantile Bank building to take a picture of the rescue of a girl trapped in a burning elevator. The only photographer making the climb, Altgens phoned in the story to his bureau before beginning the exhaustive trek back to the ground floor.[2]

Some twenty-three years after the event, Altgens recalled how he came to be at the scene of the President's assassination in 1963. "On November 21, 1963, my work assignment was in the office. While I was originally assigned to work as photo editor on November 22, I urged the assignment editor and bureau chief to let me go down to the triple underpass to make a scenic view of the presidential caravan with the Dallas skyline in the background."[3] This was an area where there was no scheduled photographic coverage. With some reluctance News Photo Editor Dave Taylor gave Altgens this requested assignment. Taylor reassigned the night photo editor to come in early and relieve Altgens.

Late that Thursday afternoon Altgens went to the Bloom Advertising Agency, which was taking care of press credentials for the presidential visit. He picked up his press identification badge which was marked "No. 196" on the back. On Friday work began early, as at 4:45 a.m., Altgens was assigned as wirephoto operator, shifting at 6:15 a.m. to cover as news photo editor.[4]

Wanting to find and be in position in plenty of time for his making photos of the motorcade, at about 11:15 a.m. Altgens walked over to the triple underpass where Main, Elm, and Commerce Streets travel under a massive concrete railroad bridge.

The Nikkorex-F Camera

Altgens brought with him his personal 35mm Nikkorex-F single-lens-reflex camera. He had purchased the camera mounted with a 50mm lens in January

1963 from Medo Photo Supply Corporation of New York, through the Associated Press. It cost $157 and was marked with serial number 371734. Today the camera body was mounted with a 105mm telephoto lens and loaded with Eastman Kodak Tri-X pan film. Altgens also carried a gadget bag with extra lenses and other camera paraphernalia. On major assignments photographers were usually given motor-driven cameras, but due to Altgens's not having been originally assigned as a photographer, he took his own hand-cocked camera, which did not lend itself to speed shooting. As Altgens knew, "This meant that what I took I had to make sure it was good – I didn't have time for second chances."[5]

James Altgens's press badge

Two uniformed police officers assigned from the Traffic Division, J. W. Foster and J. C. White, were stationed on top of the underpass. Foster came over and challenged Altgens inquiring if he was a railroad employee. Altgens said no, showed him his press tag, and explained that he had a Department of Public Safety I.D. Card, and was assigned by AP to take some photos of the motorcade. His 2¼" x 3½" white press card printed in black ink with the word "PRESS" printed below in blue was pinned to his left coat lapel. It did not help. The officer was adamant that this was private property, and that no one but railroad personnel was permitted in the area. Noting that the area seemed pretty well protected with these two cops here, and another one on the Stemmons overpass, Altgens nonetheless decided not to press the issue, and moved on to find another

photographic vantage point. The officer had not denied access to the area for security reasons, but with the fact that it was private property.[6]

Altgens walked the short distance across the overpass into the Texas School Book Depository building's parking lot, over to Elm Street at Houston, crossing Elm and traveling south on Houston over to the corner of Houston and Main Streets. To this seasoned photographer's eye, Altgens could see some potential photo opportunities as the motorcade would be traveling down the sloping grade from upper Main Street towards this point at Houston and Main. The immense "Texas Bank" roof sign was up the street on the right, and there were tall buildings on both sides of this heavily commercial district. This view might, if the building shadows did not over-contrast the light areas, make for a usable shot of the motorcade in the middle of a large Dallas crowd. The tall buildings would create a cavernous mood to the picture. After a few possible pictures here, Altgens saw that he could then run across Dealey Plaza and again catch the motorcade on Elm Street as it proceeded toward the triple underpass.[7]

It was now about 11:30 a.m. Altgens fiddled with the focus of his camera and marked time as he had done so many times before while on photographic assignment waiting for the "photo opportunity" to arrive. The crowd of spectators continued to build at this major cross-street area. Among the spectators near Altgens was Richard Oscar Bothun, an employee of the Fort Worth & Denver Railroad. Bothun was an amateur photographer who developed and printed his own black & white photos. From examining Bothun's photos and his later relocation to Elm Street, it would appear that at the time of the motorcade, the amateur mirrored Altgens's movements, either by happenstance or realizing that the professional photographer knew where to go for good shots.

At about 12:15 Altgens and many others watched as a young white man fell into an apparent epileptic seizure on

Amateur photographer Richard Bothun, from a position near Altgens, photographs the motorcade's advance cycles commanded by Sgt. S. Q. Bellah (at center) as they ride down Main Street.

Houston Street, opposite the plaza's north reflecting pool. Aided by uniformed police, the man was finally transported away in an ambulance. As the vehicle traveled down Elm Street and under the triple underpass, Altgens noticed about a dozen people on top of the railroad bridge. He thought to himself, "What the heck are all those people doing up there," at the spot where he was not allowed to stay and take his pictures. "And just as the ambulance was clearing the triple underpass, you could see the red lights as the motorcade cut onto Main Street."[8]

Rechecking his camera, Altgens could now hear the distant applause and cheers rippling closer towards him as he looked at the scene in his viewfinder. Positioning his camera at the vertical plane which best showed the tall buildings towering over the motorcade, Altgens took his first shot of the procession as it traveled toward him. He waited to make his expo- sure just at a point when the President's car hit a sunlit break between the building shadows.[9]

Contact print of Altgens's first photo

With his 105mm telephoto lens, Altgens shoots the motorcade on its way down Main Street toward his position. The lead car is at front, followed by the presidential limousine and motorcycle escort. As he makes the shot, Altgens instinctively knows this would not be the shot he wanted.

Quickly winding his camera, Altgens readied for another shot, this time with the camera at the horizontal. Waiting long enough for the lead motorcycle escort to pass his position, Altgens pushed the shutter button again, capturing the light-colored motorcade lead car in the foreground being followed by the presidential limousine and trailed closely behind by the Secret Service follow-up car.[10] Yet Altgens's instinct told him this wouldn't be the picture he wanted. Readjusting his focus, he waited for a clear view of the presidential limousine.

All around Altgens at slightly different angles, amateurs, including Richard Bothun, Phil Willis, Wilma Bond, Marie Muchmore, and Orville Nix, were taking movies and still pictures of essentially the same views as the AP photographer. Most of the amateur pictures, however, would be just slightly out of focus or were of too slow a shutter speed causing a slight blurring of features of the moving limousine and its occupants.

Waiting for the lead car to turn onto Houston and out of the camera's view, yet not waiting too long so that the motorcycles might obscure details, Altgens looked for the right moment to click. As the massive, shining blue-black Lincoln swung the corner with Secret Service driver William Greer turning the wheel, both Governor John B. and Mrs. Nellie Connally were looking towards Altgens's side of the street. He didn't even notice their glance, for the couple in the back seat were the celebrities, and the President was looking toward the camera and raising his right forearm in a wave. "Jackie Kennedy was looking at me, but the wind had just gotten up catching the First Lady's hat." She instinctively reached to hold it with her white-gloved left hand, obscuring her face to Altgens's lens.

Full-frame image of Altgens's third photo

Though Mrs. Kennedy's face was not in the picture Altgens took, the others were. So were the features of over 20 smiling spectators located across the street on the northeast corner of Houston and Main, all captured on the film in a frozen moment of time and light. Among these spectators *Dallas Morning News* artist Merle Robertson can be picked out wearing dark glasses and with a scarf around her head. She had come on her lunch break to see the motorcade. Another newspaper employee can be seen to her right. James Featherston, a reporter for the *Dallas Times Herald* was there on assignment. He was to pick up film thrown to him by Bob Jackson, a photographer in Camera Car 3 further on in the motorcade, so it could be rushed back to the paper for processing and possible use in the paper's late edition. One older woman is waving with her right hand held high, while near her another woman appears to be in the process of taking a picture of the famous American couple.[11]

This Altgens photo would, in various cropped forms, be published in hundreds of newspapers across the country within the next six hours, with the caption to the photograph alluding to the last few moments of happiness before the horror.

Cocking his camera again, Altgens took one more photo of the President's car and the trailing Secret Service Cadillac follow-up vehicle as they moved away from him and were passing the Dallas

A cropped version of the third Altgens photograph as later sent out by Associated Press.

Near Altgens's position, Bothun almost simultaneously takes this blurry photo of the turning limousine.

Altgens's fourth photo captures the limousine traveling along Houston Street toward the Book Depository.

County Criminal Courts building.[12] Grabbing his gadget bag, Altgens sprinted down the sloping grade in a northwestern direction over the grassed infield area of the Plaza. He reached the curb of the south side of Elm Street, about 240 feet from the northern corner of Elm and Houston Streets, where the motorcade was making a sharp left-hand turn. Still using his 105mm lens, since he had no time to get into his gadget bag and change lenses, Altgens had the cameras' aperture at F-11 with a shutter speed of 1/1000 of a second.[13]

Stepping off the curb into the street, Altgens looked into his viewfinder, and just a fraction of a second ahead of his clicking the shutter, he heard a noise that sounded like a firecracker going off somewhere from behind the approaching car. The noise was extraneous to Altgens and held no significance for his task. He took no notice of how many noises occurred following this first one.[14] Later estimating he was about 30 feet from the car when he took his photo, a comparison of this picture with frames from the later famous amateur film taken by spectator Abraham Zapruder indicates that it was taken around Zapruder frame #255, which would actually make Altgens's location about 60 feet from the presidential limousine.

This photograph is perhaps the most well-known of any still photograph made at the assassination scene. Along with Altgens's next photograph, it would be published in papers the world over.

Spot photographers don't typically have the benefit of time to study their subject, as things happen so quickly around them. As Altgens would vividly describe to this author at this same site some 23 years later, "My first instinct was 'well, they're shooting firecrackers up there,' or some kind of celebration on behalf of the President. And then I hear it again as the car comes on down. No one had the foggiest idea that something was taking place."[15]

His developed picture, however, showed in detail what eyes and mind could not so quickly comprehend. Because Altgens was using the 105mm telephoto lens, there is a foreshortening of features within the picture, so that people standing near the Elm and Houston Street intersection look almost the same size and distance away as people on the north side of Elm Street and the sidewalk some 120 or more feet away. In examining the photograph one can identify over 55 spectators watching the motorcade. All except two of these people and the shadows of a few more are on the north side of Elm Street. Many are still looking toward the President's car, which has by this moment passed their position, while other people have diverted their attention to the Vice-President's convertible.

Portions of the first two stories of the front northeastern side of the Texas School Book Depository are seen with at least four persons viewing the procession from the front entrance. So too, parts of three stories of the western Houston Street side of the Dal-Tex building are in view with three spectators leaning out of a second story window. Another person can be seen apparently sitting on the second floor fire escape. This man, a Black by appearance, can also be seen in Altgens's fourth photo, sitting on the fire escape. One woman to the left of the lamppost on the left side of the picture looks to be aiming a camera towards the Vice-President's convertible.[16]

Many of those spectators at the Elm and Houston Street intersection have diverted their attention completely away from the front of the motorcade, while on the extreme right of the photo the hands of Charles Brehm, who is standing about 160 feet from Houston Street, are applauding the President's appearance. While the spectators seem oblivious to anything wrong, the occupants of the President's car have had their attention diverted from these friendly onlookers. In the front seat Assistant Special Agent-in-Charge Roy H. Kellerman's face is virtually lost in shadow, while driver William R. Greer's is hidden by the flapping presidential flag. Mrs. Connally's face is also obscured, but the Governor has turned sharply to his right and seems to be wincing. The eyes and nose of President Kennedy are obscured by the limousine's rear-view mirror, but his lips appear pursed and he is cocked slightly to the left with his left arm horizontal to the plane of his mouth. His fingers are clenched. The white-gloved right hand of Mrs. Kennedy is cradling his arm. Motorcycle officer James M. Chaney, on the left side of the picture, has turned his head sharp left, while the other two visible motorcycle men seem to be looking toward the limousine.

Contact print of Altgens's fifth photo

In the "Queen Mary," the Secret Service follow-up car, driver Samuel A. Kinney and Assistant to the Special Agent-in-Charge Emory P. Roberts, both sporting dark glasses, seem to be looking toward the President. Agents John D. Ready and Paul E. Landis, on the passenger running board, are looking hard to their right, perhaps toward the sound of the report. So too, Agent George W. Hickey, Jr., situated in the back seat, is looking to his right rear. Agent Clinton J. Hill, on the driver's forward running board position, and presidential assistant Dave Powers, his forehead obscured by the rear-view mirror, seem to be looking directly at the President. In the Vice-President's Lincoln, only a glimpse of Lyndon Johnson's head can be observed, while Lady Bird's smiling face can be discerned, she sitting between her husband and Texas Senator Ralph Yarborough.

The Vice-President's Secret Service follow-up Mercury sedan vehicle is directly behind. As he had done along much of the parade route, Agent Warren W. Taylor has kept his rear passenger side door ajar in case he has to exit quickly in order to protect the Vice-President.[17] The Altgens picture captures the scene just a few seconds into the assassination of the President when, save for the victims themselves, few had had time to react to the intrusive noise they had just heard.

Still in the midst of taking his pictures and oblivious to the danger around him, Altgens stepped back onto the curb. He quickly wound his film to the next frame, adjusted his focus to 15 feet, and raised the Nikkorex to eye level, wanting a good close-up of the President and Mrs. Kennedy. The limousine came towards him at about 11 mph, and as it passed just about 15 feet to the front of him, and as he was about ready to snap the picture, Altgens heard another report.

A high-velocity bullet punctured the rear of the President's head. "Fragments of his head fell right at my feet. That was some heck of an explosion when it hit his head. His skull just disintegrated and bone and flesh flying." The horror was unexpected. Kennedy's head was covered with blood. According to Altgens, "It stunned me so at what I saw, that I failed to do my duty and make the picture that I was trying to make." Mrs. Kennedy then grabbed the President and Altgens heard her cry, "Oh, no!" as his body slumped over into her lap. Altgens also heard on the radio from within the car, "We've been hit, get us to the nearest hospital," the words coming out, as Altgens emphasized, "loud and clear."[18]

Speaking of the event over two decades later, Altgens's memory was still vivid of the horror of the moment and the later criticism by some. "The big showdown came at the time J.F.K. received the shot to the head. I had prefocused, had my hand on the trigger, but when J.F.K.'s head exploded, sending substance in my direction, I virtually became paralyzed. This was such a shock to me that I never did press the trigger on the camera. The sight was unbelievable, and I was surprised I recovered fast enough to make the picture of the Secret Service man aiding Mrs. Kennedy.

This, to me, was an awesome experience. Yet, many news people say I should have taken the picture anyway, regardless of the circumstances. Perhaps they are right. Nevertheless, they must put themselves in the identical, same position before they criticize."

When, on a day shy of the twenty-third anniversary of the assassination, Altgens revisited his original location at Dealey Plaza with this author, he again tried to convey the horror and, at the same time, his frustration concerning this missed photo. "I really can't tell you in a way that anyone will truly understand. But to have a president shot to death right in front of you – and keep your cool, and do what you're supposed to do – I'm not real sure that the most seasoned photographers would be able to do it. . . . It's not that I'm looking for any excuse, it's just that there is no excuse for this. I should have made the picture I was set up to make. And I didn't do it."[19]

The photographer's shock and disbelief at such a ghastly sight was momentary, and the veteran's instinct took hold. Altgens stepped out to the curb and aimed his camera at the now quickly accelerating presidential vehicle. He shot a forlorn scene in which agent Clint Hill is on the limousine rear step. Mrs. Kennedy, who in her shock had attempted to grab a piece of the President's head which had landed on the trunk, is moving back into the car. The white lead car is a few lengths ahead, just starting into the shadow of the underpass on which some ten spectators, including signal supervisor S. M. Holland second from left, can be seen peering down at the horror taking place below.[20]

With the presidential Lincoln disappearing within the underpass, Altgens made a picture of the activity across Elm Street showing amateur movie maker Abraham Zapruder and his secretary Marilyn Sitzman just after they had gotten down from the concrete wall from where

Altgens shoots this forlorn scene of the limousine approaching the triple underpass right after the assassination.

Altgens takes his last photo from the south side of Elm toward the colonnade area. He then crosses over to that side.

After Altgens crosses Elm Street, Richard Bothun also makes a picture of the colonnade area. Altgens is seen at left.

he had filmed the assassination. In the middle of the frame are spectators Mr. and Mrs. Charles Hester hunkered down in front of the colonnade area.[21]

Altgens quickly crossed the street. The area was in "utter confusion" as uniformed policemen went racing up the incline of the "grassy knoll." Says Altgens about the scene, "Well, I thought they were on to something. I was satisfied that the shot came from the rear, but I didn't know where in the rear. So I figured they had spotted the guy somewhere and they had chased him up here, and I wanted to come over and get a picture of the guy – if they had such a person in custody. And I came over here and by the time I can get up to the hill, they're turned around and are coming back. And they hadn't found anything."[22]

Altgens then took a "good look" around the area to see that no one else had been shot. He observed a family of four sprawled out on the ground. The parents, Gail and Bill Newman, were protectively covering their two children. Some of the cameramen from the motorcade had in the meantime jumped out of their vehicles and were scurrying to this area, taking pictures as they approached.

From across Elm Street, near Altgens's position at the time of the shooting, amateur photographer Richard Bothun took a picture of the scene. Bothun had apparently followed Altgens when he had rushed from Houston Street to the south side of Elm. Although he had not made any pictures during the assassination due to his own shock at the shot hitting the President's head, Bothun now captured on film a view of motorcade cycle officer Bobby W. Hargis traveling down Elm Street. Altgens is on the opposite side of Elm Street, at camera left, standing near the Newman family, having just returned back down the grass slope.[23]

Several others also took pictures of the dramatic scene of the Newman family on the ground. One of these photographers Altgens knew well. Donald C.

Altgens's brother-in-law, Clint Grant, takes this view of the colonnade from the second camera car. Altgens stands at the curb at right. The west side of the Book Depository building is visible in the right background.

"Clint" Grant, Sr., was traveling in the motorcade as a photographer for the *Dallas Morning News* in the second camera car. Grant, a World War II veteran who had earned the rank of captain and possessed five battle stars, had joined the staff of the *Morning News* after the war. He had been the only local photographer to accompany the President from the point of origin in Washington, D.C., for the entire Texas trip. Grant was married to Myrtis Halliburton, Jim Altgens's wife Clara's sister. The two professional photographers were brothers-in-law.

An accomplished news photographer, Grant was also well known in the Dallas area for his photos of children and animals. A number of his pictures had been published in *LIFE* magazine and in other national periodicals. This Texas trip with the President was the first assignment on which Grant was using a smaller 35mm negative format camera, and he carried with him two Nikon F's, one mounted with a 35mm and the other with a 105mm lens. Grant described what happened at the time of the shooting from his vantage point aboard the convertible, located as the seventh car behind the President's. "Driving down Main Street, we had just turned onto Houston Street when we heard one shot – pause – two shots in rapid succession. I thought it was someone playing a prank – maybe a kid's cherry bomb. Consequently, I gave it no more thought until we turned onto Elm Street and saw all the people prone on the ground."[24]

As Grant's car passed by the activity on the north side of Elm Street, he made one photo showing the Newmans on the ground with CBS's Tom Craven running along the sidewalk, trailed by White House cameraman Tom Atkins. There on the sidewalk by the curb was Grant's brother-in-law, Jim Altgens, who unlike all the other press and photographers traveling in the motorcade, actually knew that the President had been frightfully struck by assassination. Momentarily pausing before finding a gap in the procession to scurry across the street, Altgens glances at his brother-in-law in the slowly moving convertible. After a few moments at the curbside, Altgens is able to re-cross Elm Street and retrieve his gadget bag. "My main concern from that point on was getting my stuff back to the office."[25]

Realizing the extreme importance of what he had seen and the pictures he had taken, Altgens sprinted back to the Dallas Morning News building. Part of the way he was in the company of WFAA-TV personality Jerry Haynes. Altgens caught the correct signal lights at each intersection and even an elevator waiting on the first floor. Arriving at the third floor AP wirephoto office, he picked up the interoffice phone which rang automatically in the news office. Dallas AP Bureau Chief Robert H. Johnson, Jr., came on the line to hear Altgens blurt out, "Bob, the President has been shot!"

"Ike, how do you know?" Johnson incredulously asked. "I saw it, there was blood on his head, Jackie jumped up and grabbed him and cried, 'Oh, no!' The motorcade raced onto the Freeway."

"Ike, you saw that?" cried Johnson.

And Altgens affirmed, "Yes, I was shooting pictures and then I saw it."

Johnson yelled "Bulletin!" as he typed the most important lines of his career. Night Editor Ron Thompson pulled the bulletin from the typewriter and quickly handed it to wire operator Julia Saunders. At 12:39 Central Standard Time the bulletin was on the wire. "Dallas, Nov. 22 (AP) – President Kennedy was shot today just as his motorcade left downtown Dallas. Mrs. Kennedy jumped up and grabbed Mr. Kennedy. She cried 'Oh, No!' The motorcade sped on." The bulletin was received in newsrooms and government offices throughout the nation. One of the first public media outlets to broadcast the AP report was Dallas TV station WFAA, which interrupted its regular programming to begin coverage at about 12:45. Program Director Jay Watson read the shocking news from a quickly rushed-in bulletin – "An Associated Press photographer, James

Altgens, reports he saw blood on the President's head. The AP man said he heard two shots, but thought someone was shooting fireworks, until he saw blood on the President. He also said he saw no one with a gun."[26]

Altgens remembers that while the bulletin was being readied, "Someone grabbed my camera, removed the film and took it in to process it, because they wanted me on the telephone reporting what I saw. We did an extraordinary good job, because within 20 minutes of the assassination we had a picture rolling on the wire – and that's good. All the wires were connected together, which means they got it in Africa and London, all over the world, at the same time that people got it in the U. S. of A. It was fantastic. I saw some of the cable photos that came back in that night, and one or more of the pictures I had taken were on page one of many of the world newspapers."[27]

The photo caption of the motorcade under fire, one of three Altgens photos sent out on the wirephoto network, read: "(DN2) DALLAS, TEX., NOV. 22 – KENNEDY SHOT IN DALLAS – President John F. Kennedy was shot today just as his motorcade left downtown Dallas. He was taken to Parkland Hospital. Secret Service men are looking from where the shots came from (AP Wirephoto) (cel61303 stf – jwa) 1963." The AP photo code at the sign-off indicated that Carl E. Linde (cel) was the caption writer, 6 indicated the day was Friday, 1303 that it was sent at 1:03 p.m., and the photo was taken by staff member James W. Altgens.[28]

Staying long enough to provide identification of what he had photographed, Altgens relates that, "After my pictures cleared the wirephoto network, I was sent to Parkland Hospital to work with AP Washington photographer Henry Burroughs. We stayed until President Kennedy's body was removed from the hospital to *Air Force One* at Love Field. I then was sent back to the assassination site to make photos that could be diagrammed. I later was sent to City Hall to pick up photos

made by photographer Ted Powers and bring the film back to our office to process. These were pictures made of Oswald in police custody, and this was the first and only time I saw Oswald." Altgens got a glimpse of the assassination suspect as Lee Oswald was being taken from the interrogation room at Police Headquarters to another room. To Altgens, the accused looked exhausted, "Like they had put him through the interrogation ringer."[29]

A little after 5:00 p.m. Altgens returned to Dealey Plaza and took a series of 21 photographs of the Book Depository, triple underpass, and pictures from the point where he had taken his first photo of the motorcade under fire. Altgens's original negatives of the motorcade were sent to Associated Press headquarters via an airline pilot on a commercial flight to New York, where a special messenger picked them up and delivered them to the AP office.[30] Altgens had been so busy, that he had not gotten prints of his photos and had to request copies from New York, but apparently he never acquired a whole set of his pictures.

In later years Altgens became unsure of the number of photographs he took that day of the assassination, and has been reluctant to acknowledge photo credit of all seven since he is very adamant about not wanting to take credit for someone else's work. In discussions with him, it is evident that he is sure or reasonably sure that he took five of the photos, but admits to leaving things to AP's judgment. In testimony six months after the shooting, he did mention that he made one or two pictures of the caravan coming down Main Street, but with the length of intervening years and the fact that he possibly never saw in print form all his pictures before the negatives were sent to New York, this explains some of his caution about authorship of the photos.

An examination of the negative sequence, however, shows quite conclusively that these seven pictures are Altgens's, a fact first noticed by researcher Richard E. Sprague, who found the indi-

In this blow-up of the doorway portion of Altgens's assassination photograph, Billy Lovelady (in circle) resembled Lee Oswald enough to make this Altgens photo the subject of much speculation.

vidually cut negatives at AP in New York. The film is of the same type (Tri-X), is numbered sequentially, is chronological, and taken from the same vantage points at which Altgens is known to have been located. Mr. Altgens's personal caution is refreshing, but in light of the evidence, not problematical to the evidence.

Although the published photographs that were circulated all over the nation and world clearly showed that an AP photographer was present at the assassination, no government official contacted Altgens or the Dallas AP about the events the photographer had witnessed. Altgens tried to get his bureau chief to give him permission to notify the authorities to let them know he had been in the area, but his boss never got permission for him. Altgens did not feel he had the authority to act on his own. Yet, although the official investigations resulting from the President's

murder seemed uninterested in finding Altgens for his account, others were very interested in one of his pictures.

A number of people spotted the uncanny resemblance of accused assassin Lee Harvey Oswald to one of the men standing in the doorway of the Book Depository building, as seen in Altgens's fifth photo. If this man watching the motorcade was Oswald, how could he be accused of simultaneously shooting the President from an upper window? Three days after the assassination, Mike Shapiro, manager of WFAA-TV in Dallas, brought this observation to the attention of the FBI. He stated that, ". . . an individual in the Associated Press office at Pittsburgh, Pennsylvania, had noticed the similarities between the individual in the doorway and Lee Harvey Oswald."[31]   Others also noticed. Mrs. Helen Shirah of Jacksonville, Florida, wrote to the Secret Service in January

In 1971 photographer Bob Jackson posed Lovelady in front of the School Book Depository wearing the same shirt as on November 22, 1963. At a distance of 8 years and with Lovelady having lost hair, grown sideburns, and gained weight, it was still evident he was one and the same as the 1963 figure.

1964, pointing out the man "who bears a striking resemblance to Lee Harvey Oswald," from a photo in a magazine she had purchased. Stating that she was sure they were very thorough in their investigation, "... and had probably checked out all available pictures...," Mrs. Shirah had no idea of how cavalier the investigation was with actually gathering photographic evidence.[32]

Lovelady in 1964.

In this instance, however, the FBI was checking out this troubling identity question. On November 25 agents had interviewed Roy S. Truly, warehouse manager of the Book Depository, who identified the person in the doorway as employee Billy Nolan Lovelady. Agents also spoke to Lovelady, who confirmed he was indeed the person in the picture and admitted to them that there was a resemblance between Oswald and himself. Lovelady would later tell an interviewer that when the agents had shown him the Altgens picture, "Right away I pointed to me and they seemed relieved. One had a big smile on his face because it wasn't Oswald. They said they had a big discussion down at the FBI and one guy said it just had to be Oswald."[33]

On January 30, 1964, Assistant Manager William H. Shelley was also interviewed. He stated that the person in the photo was Lovelady and that he, Shelley, had been standing next to Lovelady that day during the assassination.[34]

Although critics of the 1964 Warren Commission investigation continued for years to question the identity of the man at the Depository entrance, spurred on by a mix-up of what shirt Lovelady was wearing that day, the evidence is quite overwhelming that the man was Lovelady. This conclusion was only strengthened as a result of the investigative work of the House Select Committee on Assassinations in 1978.[35]

The question of the identity of the man in the Altgens photo aside, investigators had not apparently even attempted to find and interview Altgens, a witness to the assassination who might shed light upon other important matters. On May 11 and 14, 1964, Altgens received phone calls at his home from a Dom Bonafede, who was preparing a story on the controversial Altgens photograph.[36]

The resulting Bonafede article was published in the magazine section of the *New York Herald Tribune* on May 24, 1964, under the title "The Picture with a Life of Its Own," referring to the Oswald look-alike. Bonafede described the Altgens photo as "the Classic assassination photo," and noted that even though the photographer could recall the shooting in great detail, Altgens had never been questioned by the FBI. The following day a column by Maggie Daly, "Daly Diary," published in the *Chicago American* asked: "Isn't it odd that J. W. Altgens, a veteran Associated Press photographer in Dallas, who took a picture of the Kennedy Assassination – one of the witnesses close enough to see the President shot and able to describe second-by-second what happened – has been questioned neither by the FBI nor the Warren Commission?"[37] The Chicago FBI reported this column to Washington. Finally and undoubtedly as a result of critical comment by the press, on June 2, 1964, over six months after the assassination, Altgens was finally interviewed by an FBI agent, resulting in a five-page report.

On July 22, 1964, Wesley J. Liebeler, Assistant Counsel for the Warren Commission, took testimony from Altgens at the Dallas Post Office building. According to the record, the testimony amounted to nine printed pages, and took only some 15 minutes to conduct. Liebeler centered his questioning on the circumstances of Altgens taking his photographs, his movement in the Plaza, the number, spacing, and direction of the gun shots, his distance from the limousine, and questions relating to Altgens's ability to identify anyone in his well known fifth photograph. The testimony reads as non-confrontational and Altgens comes off as a cooperative witness feeling somewhat guilty of not stepping forward to make the authorities aware of his presence at the assassination and wishing that he had been able to give his testimony when it was fresh in his mind.[38]

Until the news stories about their negligence surfaced, the investigative bodies made no effort to contact Altgens. Instead of actively seeking out this man who had obviously been an important witness to the killing, the government had to be prodded into action by newspaper questions.

There is no evidence to show that the original negatives or first generation full frame prints were requested or obtained by the FBI or Warren Commission, save for their use of cropped Associated Press wirephoto prints of his fifth photograph of the series. All this is consistent with the cavalier attitude on the part of the government towards potential photographic evidence during the entire 1963-1964 official investigation into the assassination.

In 1969 at the time of the New Orleans trial of businessman Clay Shaw on the charge of conspiracy in the death of President Kennedy, Altgens received a subpoena from District Attorney Jim Garrison's office to appear as a trial witness. Altgens, having read about the controversial investigation, was not eager to become involved. "I really didn't want to go, because Garrison's reputation had already been pretty well established, and most of the things that he was doing were self-aggrandizement." Altgens was concerned that given the reputation of the DA's investigation, the photographer's testimony might be badly twisted. A subpoena from another state jurisdiction had to be examined by a Texas state court to judge if it should or should not be honored. Altgens appeared before Judge Holland's court with a copy of one of his photos, and an explanation that the picture and his testimony before the Warren Commission attorney was the sum and substance of his information. He voiced his reluctance to the judge about going to Louisiana, but the judge nonetheless told Altgens he thought he ought to go and urged the photographer to, "have a fun time in New Orleans."[39]

Several weeks later a check for $300 for plane fare to New Orleans arrived with a notice that he would be contacted when to make the trip. "About a week or two later, when I was down in Houston, I happened to run into John Connally. I had known him from past times when I had to cover him in office, and also had been out at his ranch a time or two." Asking of Connally's health, the former governor responded that he was pretty well, although the wrist that had been shot through during the assassination still hurt him quite a bit. Altgens asked him if he too had received a subpoena from Garrison. The governor replied, "Oh Hell yes! But I'm not going." Connally decried Garrison and the standing of his case, remarking that he had cashed his travel expense check and spent it. He urged Altgens do the same, which advice was soon thereafter taken. Later it was reported by the press that Governor Connally and James Altgens of AP would not be called to testify in the Shaw trial, as they were hostile witnesses. Thus ended Altgens's connection with the Garrison case.[40]

"Ike" Altgens took early retirement from Associated Press in September of 1979 in lieu of a transfer, wanting to remain in his native Dallas. Working a number of years as a field representative of Ford Motor Company for their display and exhibit department, Altgens was often sought out by assassination buffs for his recollections. He freely conceded that, ". . . there will always be some controversy about details surrounding the site and shooting of the President," but wondered whether at this point in time it is possible to uncover something that investigators have overlooked. He always said he had yet to see indisputable evidence to the contrary that Oswald did not kill the President.[41]

Ever a polite and affable gentleman possessing a sense of history and enjoying the sharing of stories of his varied and interesting career, Altgens was forever careful not to embellish his recollections. Emphasizing, "I don't have any authority to speak about something of which I don't know," Altgens did not suffer gladly the eyewitnesses to November 22, 1963, who changed and embellished their stories over the years. He was bemused and perplexed by many of the conspiracy theorists who spent much of their time devising intricate scenarios and who attempted to convince him, with detailed diagrams and rambling letters, that what he had seen and experienced was incorrect and what they imagined is the truth. "Until those people come up with solid evidence to support their claims, I see no value in wasting my time with them." Both Mr. and Mrs. Altgens passed away at their Dallas home in December 1995.[42]

The original Altgens negatives which were created on November 22, 1963, are deposited with other negatives on the subject within the vast Wide World Photo operations in New York City. Some of the original seven negatives have had copy negatives in cropped format created, while others of this historically valuable set unfortunately appear to be misidentified, misplaced, or even missing.

CHAPTER NOTES

1. "Lone 'Pro' On Scene Where JFK Was Shot," *Editor and Publisher*, 12/7/1963, p. 11, 61; *Hearings Before the President's Commission on the Assassination of President Kennedy*, v. 7, p. 516; Altgens interview with Trask, 11/21/1985, 10/23/1992.
2. "Lone," op. cit., p. 61.; Altgens interview, 11/21/1985; Altgens obituary, *Dallas Morning News*, 12/15/1995; Film, "Beyond the Time Barrier, " 1960. Altgens would also appear as a witness, though not as himself, in the 1964 film, "The Trial of Lee Harvey Oswald."
3. Letter, Altgens to Trask, 3/31/1984.

4. Ibid.; Letter, Altgens to Trask, 6/21/1986; "Lone," op. cit., p. 11.
5. Letter, Altgens to Trask, 6/23/1984; Letter, Altgens to Trask, 6/21/1986.
6. *Hearings*, op. cit., v. 6, p. 249-50; v.7, p. 516.
7. Ibid., v. 7, p. 516-517.
8. Ibid., v. 7, p. 524; Altgens interview, 11/21/1985.
9. Altgens photograph 11/22/1963, roll 1, #2. First photograph in the series was frame #2.
10. Ibid., roll 1, #3.
11. Ibid., roll 1, #4; Altgens interview, 11/21/1985.
12. Ibid., roll 1, #5. This photograph was the subject of speculation by some critics who believed it pictured among the spectators on Houston Street, Joseph A. Milteer, a right-wing organizer alleged to have been a possible conspirator. In the late 1970s consultants for the House Select Committee made a study of this photograph (*Appendix to Hearings Before the Select Committee*, v. 6, p. 242-257) which study supported the conclusion that the man was not Milteer.
13. *Hearings*, op. cit., v. 22, p. 790; "Lone," op. cit., p. 11; Altgens interview, 11/21/1985.
14. *Hearings*, op. cit., v. 7, p. 517-518.
15. Altgens interview, 11/21/1985.
16. Altgens photograph, op. cit., roll 1, #6. Several researchers noticed in this Altgens photograph a rifle-shaped object protruding out of the second floor of the Dal-Tex building at the fire escape landing. Indeed, some claimed to see this as a rifle with silencer, together with a pillow propped on one of the metal fire escape steps. Robert J. Groden, a critic who served as a consultant to the HSCA photography panel, examined the original negative of this photograph and reported that "using my technique of vario-density cynexing, I was able to enhance the image in the window to the point of clarity where the figure in the window is now identifiable as a black man leaning on the window sill with both hands, and with no gun in view." (*HSCA* v.6, p. 307.)
17. *Hearings*, op. cit., v. 18, p. 777, 782. A number of researchers have noted the VP follow-up car's open door and have explained it as evidence of a quick response of the Vice-President's protectors, in contrast to the President's agents. Some others have seen in this super-fast reaction a sinister foreknowledge of the event. These explanations are examples of persons reading more into photographs than is necessarily there. Agent Taylor's report of his activities indicated, and photos taken earlier in the motorcade, including a picture by Cecil Stoughton in Camera Car 2 of the motorcade on Main Street, as well as a film sequence made by Marie Muchmore of the motorcade on Houston Street, revealed that this door was ajar during much, if not all, of the motorcade.
18. Ibid., v. 7, p. 518; v. 22, p. 791; Altgens interview, 11/21/1985.
19. Letter, Altgens to Trask, 6/23/1984; Altgens interview, 11/21/1985; Letter, Altgens to Trask, 6/21/1986. In a 1993 letter Altgens mentioned he recalled not seeing any blood on the right side or face of the President which was obscured to him. ". . . But there was plenty of blood on the left side and rear of his head. I noticed this as he slowly fell down onto the seat next to Jackie Kennedy." (Letter, Altgens to Trask, 8/11/1993.)
20. Altgens photograph, op. cit., roll 1, #7. During the assassination S. M. Holland noticed what he described as a "puff of smoke" in front of the stockade fence area on the grassy knoll. Feeling that a shot had originated from that location, he and two companions went to the area to see if they could find something.
21. Ibid., roll 1, #8.
22. Altgens interview, 11/21/1985.
23. Richard Bothun Elm Street photograph, 11/22/1963.
24. Letter, Clint Grant to Trask, 12/1/1987; Letter, Grant to Trask, 1/6/1988.
25. Clint Grant Elm Street photograph, 11/22/1963; Altgens interview, 11/21/1985.
26. Bob Johnson, "Too Busy for Tears," *The AP World*, 8/1972, p. 18-19; *The Torch is Passed*, p. 14; Altgens interview, 11/21/1985; WFAA-TV coverage, 12:45-12:48 p.m. CST, 11/22/1963.
27. Altgens interview, 11/21/1985.
28. AP Wirephoto caption "cel61303stf-jwa," 11/22/1963; Letter, Altgens to Trask, 6/21/1986.
29. Letter, Altgens to Trask, 3/31/1984; Letter, Altgens to Trask, 4/21/1984.
30. Letter, Altgens to Trask, 3/31/1984.
31. Harold Weisberg, *Photographic Whitewash*, p. 188. By December 2 Associated Press distributed an enlargement of this Altgens photo to its subscribers with a circle around the mystery man. Titled "Photo arouses new interest," the caption concluded with the fact: "Authorities said the man in the picture is not Oswald but another employee of the Depository." (*New York Herald Tribune Magazine*, 5/24/1964, p. 9.)
32. Ibid., p. 189-191.
33. Ibid., p. 189, 191-192; *New York Herald Tribune Magazine*, 5/24/1964, p. 10.
34. Weisberg, op. cit., p. 191. Altgens was later contacted by Lovelady, via telephone, who requested a copy of this famous photograph. Altgens was happy to comply, but could not secure from the elusive Lovelady an interview or photo session. He was told by Mrs. Lovelady, whom he met shortly afterwards, that Lovelady's elusiveness was due not so much to the assassination's events, as to threats on himself and his wife's children by a former husband, whom the family was attempting to avoid. By November 1971 *Dallas Times Herald* photographer Bob Jackson was able to have a photo session with Lovelady. Wearing the same shirt he'd had on the day of the assassination, Lovelady posed on the steps of the Book Depository building for several copyrighted pictures. (*Dallas Times Herald* photograph files, JFK #9, now located among the Dallas history collection of the Dallas Public Library, MA 93.5/303 & 304.)
35. *New York Times*, 5/24/1964, p. 7; *Appendix to Hearings Before the Select Committee on Assassinations*, v. 6, p. 286-293.
36. *Hearings*, op. cit., v. 22, p. 791-792.
37. *Chicago American*, 5/25/1964, p. 7.
38. *Hearings*, op. cit., v. 7, p. 517-525.
39. Altgens interview, 10/23/1992.
40. Ibid.
41. Letter, Altgens to Trask, 4/21/1984, 6/23/1984.
42. Altgens interview, 11/16/1991, 10/23/1992; Letter, Altgens to Trask,12/19/1991; Altgens obituary, op. cit.

The Free-Lancer

Free-lance photographer and film maker Jim Murray had not expected to take any pictures of the President's visit to Dallas on the 22nd of November. Indeed, his viewing of the motorcade and the President was not a matter of pre-planning, but rather that of casual timing. Murray never did take any pictures of the fateful motorcade, but because of his chance proximity to the scene of the assassination, he ended up recording more photographic frames of the confused aftermath at Dealey Plaza than any other photographer that day.

~

Jim Murray interviews Senator Kennedy in 1957.

In 1963 Jim Murray was a 34-year-old husband and father of two children. Born in Rockford, Illinois, on September 9, 1929, Murray had moved to Texas as a teenager. He had attended the Universities of Missouri, Houston, and Arizona, and graduated in 1954 from Southern Methodist University in Dallas, earning a degree in journalism. Possessing a casual interest in photography, Murray learned to work in both still and motion picture formats after going to work in the Dallas bureau of Fort Worth television station WBAP. From 1955 to 1960 he worked out of the press room of the Dallas County Criminal Courts building, across Houston Street from Dealey Plaza. On November 28, 1957, WBAP-TV assigned Murray to interview the junior senator from Massachusetts when John Kennedy was traveling through Dallas. Having been nominated and considered as a serious contender for the vice-presidential slot at the 1956 Democratic party convention, the youthful Kennedy was a rising star within the nation's political scene.

Performing all the film interview tasks himself, Murray set up his camera equipment and placed Kennedy in a bench seat at the American Airlines airport lounge at Dallas's Love Field. He then sat down himself with microphone in hand and conducted the interview, reaching out to the camera several times to adjust the lens. Murray questioned the senator about his political future, asking if he would accept a draft at the 1960 convention. He also inquired if Kennedy believed his youthfulness was a political asset or liability. Kennedy responded with evasive charm that his immediate political future was to run for re-election to the Senate in 1958, and that whatever asset or liability youth is, time has a way of dealing with it. In September 1960, during that year's presidential campaign, Murray again filmed John Kennedy when the now presidential candidate toured the San Antonio, Texas area.[1]

Murray had moved the 270 miles to San Antonio in August 1960, first employed as assistant news director for KENS-TV, and later working as a free-lancer, doing magazine still photography as well as motion picture assignments. Around the beginning of November 1963, the Murrays had moved back to Dallas where business prospects for a free-lancer were brighter. On Saturday, November 23,

Jim was scheduled to film a Southern Methodist University football game for Dallas television station WFAA, highlights of which would be packaged for a day-after broadcast. Deciding to check out the station's film equipment in preparation for the next day, Murray went in the late morning of November 22 to WFAA, located at Communications Center only a few blocks southeast of Dealey Plaza. He arrived there at about the time President Kennedy was landing at Love Field, and watched some of the live airport coverage on a monitor at the station.

As Murray had no assignment to photograph the President's visit, and since he knew that the event would be thoroughly covered by the press, Murray figured a salable free-lance photo would be a remote possibility. Ironically, had he been on an "assignment," he likely would have been somewhere other than near Dealey Plaza, which was at the tag end of the downtown motorcade route. The best photo opportunities would have been elsewhere. He didn't think there was any point in making personal snapshots of the arrival and motorcade, and a brief glimpse of Kennedy in a parade was not a high priority.[2]

Murray was, however, an unqualified "supporter" of the President, and although he would not go out of his way to see the motorcade, he was close to where it was scheduled to pass by. The County Sheriff's office was located at the Dallas County Criminal Courts building on the northeast corner of Houston and Main Streets. The County Press Room was in this building, and Murray had worked out of this room for some five years prior to his move to San Antonio. As he knew most of the local reporters as well as people in the sheriff's office, Murray decided it would be an opportune time to renew old acquaintances and incidentally get a chance to see the motorcade.

Driving to the Plaza area, Murray noted that the parking spaces on the main streets were off-limits due to the motorcade route. He found a space on Houston Street by the rear loading dock of the Texas School Book Depository building, probably parking illegally, but figuring that the police would be too busy working the parade to write up parking tickets on streets off the parade route. In the trunk of his 1959 Ford, Murray had left his two Asahi Pentax 35mm cameras. The black-bodied cameras were relatively new, having been purchased by mail from Hong Kong in 1961. In retrospect, Murray regrets not thinking to carry his cameras with him. There was an undercurrent of uneasiness about the President's visit. Dallas was a hotbed of right-wing politics, and city officials had gone out of their way to urge citizens to refrain from any embarrassing incident that would mar the Kennedy visit. But that the President could be murdered on a downtown street was simply beyond comprehension.[3]

While at the sheriff's office, Murray remembers engaging in conversation about the day's events. A woman remarked how nice it was that the weather was now so good that they could take the bubble-top off of the presidential Lincoln. Murray, like scores of others on the scene that day, noticed a man on Houston Street who went into a seizure, and the commotion it generated a few minutes prior to the motorcade's arrival. He watched the motorcade through windows on the first floor of the Criminal Courts building, first from the corner window facing on Main Street, and then as the cars turned on to Houston Street, switching his view to the west-facing windows. As the Lincoln passed under Murray's window, he recalls observing Mrs. Kennedy leaning towards the President. With a noticeable frown on her face, she made a brief and private comment to her husband, before resuming her smiles to the cheering crowd. Murray remembers thinking it appeared that for the First Lady, motorcades were not a pleasure – just a tiresome duty.

I watched the vehicles till they turned back down [Elm] towards the triple underpass, and at that point they were very quickly lost to my

Amateur photographer Phil Willis snaps a picture of the presidential limousine on Houston Street. In the left background is the Criminal Courts building. Jim Murray is watching from the corner window. Arrow points to Vice-President Johnson.

line of sight behind that cement grillwork on the Plaza. They were then out of my sight and I heard what I didn't recognize as gunshots. . . . What I heard were three reports, and there was a longer pause between the first and second than the second and third. And at the same time, or immediately afterwards, I saw running up the embankment, the infamous "grassy slope," what I think were teenagers. And I thought, "Teenagers have thrown firecrackers at the motorcade – Dallas has got more egg on its face."

Being a photographic free-lancer aware of a potential transitory though salable spot news photo, Murray figured if he acted fast he might shoot a picture at the scene which could be captioned something like, "Teenagers Collared by Cops." Running out the back door of the Sheriff's Department, Murray raced to his car and opened up the trunk. "I had a roll of Kodachrome in at least one of my cameras, and a roll of Kodachrome was several dollars which I couldn't afford to waste. And if you were thinking in terms of a news photo that would more quickly run on a wire service, Kodachrome [color] was not very useful because it couldn't be processed quickly. So I swapped out, rolled it back and put black & white film in both cameras. Again, I was not thinking in terms of the biggest news story I would ever cover. The murder of a President within earshot was simply unimaginable."

The teenagers Murray saw were undoubtedly two boys who were standing on the north side of Elm Street near the John Chism family, watching the procession, and who, when the shots were fired, ran up the incline to the northeast concrete shelter. Shortly thereafter, they ran down the slope in a southwesterly direction and were captured, together with another running youth, in several photographs taken by *Fort Worth Star Telegram* photographer Harry Cabluck from aboard a press bus in the motorcade.[4]

Murray estimates it took him about three minutes after hearing the three reports to get to his car and prepare his cameras. With the two cameras around his neck, he quickly moved to the Elm and Houston street corner near the Book Depository's front entrance. "The first thing that attracted my attention was a couple of black women holding on to each other, sobbing. It was obviously a scene worth shooting, but it struck me as hysterical; an overwrought response to what I still believed was a minor incident involving teenagers and firecrackers. The crowd seemed stunned and milled around without direction. There was no visible focus to the activity."

A problem arose trying to snap this shot. In three of Murray's first four film frames, his camera jammed with the shutter open. This was a result of a mismated 55mm automatic lens. The frames were completely over-exposed. The first good exposure shows the two black women clutching one another, one crying and the other holding a portable radio. The scene captured on film is a picture of confusion. Ten other spectators, including a cop and two men in hard-hats, are looking in various directions. A black woman on the right of the frame has a troubled look and is gazing toward Murray while caressing her chin with her right hand. Another woman in the left background also has a hand to her face. Murray snapped this shot near the north finger of land adjacent to Elm Street and Elm Street Extension. To the rear can be seen the two bottom floors of the Dal-Tex building. Author Josiah Thompson, in his 1967 book *Six Seconds in Dallas*, reproduced three of Murray's photographs, including a cropped version of this one, identifying one of the hard-hat men as Howard Brennan. According to Thompson's description, Brennan is looking up "... at the Depository window where minutes before he had seen an assassin take his last shot."[5] At the time of the shooting Brennan was sitting on a concrete retaining wall on the south side of Elm Street and was facing the Depository. Shortly after this photo was taken, Brennan told officer William Barnett, also visible in the photo, that he had seen the assassin fire from the sixth-story corner window.

Murray's next attempted photo failed again due to the mismated mechanism. It was at this point that he switched-out the problem lens for a 35mm wide-angle lens. "I sort of worked my way off that corner, down toward the site of the grassy knoll, and the news became worse at every step." Moving westerly along the dirt Elm Street Extension road into a railroad parking area, Murray squeezed off two pictures, the first including in its view the north tower of the Union Terminal Railroad.

The second photo Murray made here was taken at the rear of the north pergola, near a parking curb composed of railroad ties. The view included the open-grid metal railroad signal gantry in the background. In the foreground of both pictures are parked cars and numerous people milling around, many looking at the ground. A number of these people had run up the knoll facing Elm Street seeking the assassin's location. All this activity and tramping around only made a search for potential clues nearly impossible.

Turning to the east, Murray then made a picture of the Elm Street Extension road with part of the front and west side of the Book Depository visible to the left. A large crowd is gathered in front of a paneled truck, while others are walking back towards the Depository. Photographic researcher Richard Sprague later identified the Dallas police officer standing near the parked police cruiser at the left as Elvin M. Perdue, with Sam Webster behind him.[6] Knowing some of the law officers who were in the crowd, Murray soon learned that something terrible had occurred. "It wasn't until I worked my way west on the Elm Street Extension, behind the grassy

Murray takes his first photo near the corner of Elm and Houston Streets.

As a cop looks over the area from the top of a railroad car, civilians walk among parked cars.

Assassinaton witnesses Amos Euins and Hugh Betzner are among those wandering around the parking lot.

An eastern view up the dirt Elm Street Extension toward the front door of the Book Depository building.

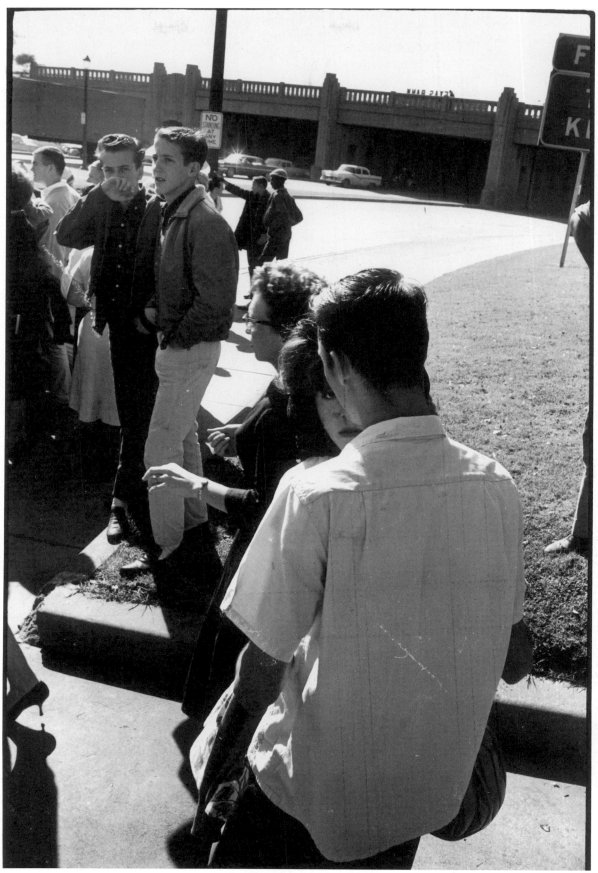

People cluster about the sidewalk on the north side of Elm Street. In the background is the triple underpass.

A view of the crowd clustered around Elm Street. In the background is the eastern end of Dealey Plaza. Cars are now traveling on the location on Elm Street where minutes earlier a President of the United States had been slain.

knoll, talking to witnesses, that the enormity of the event began to hit home, one fact at a time."

"Yes, there were gunshots!"

"Yes, the President was hit!"

"Yes, he was hit bad!"

Murray describes his next 20 minutes or so as "walking around in a daze that this could have happened," and "shooting randomly without any specific direction." Any time that afternoon that he saw activity, he made a picture. Murray left the railroad yard area and traveled south to the area of the grassy knoll. Taking four additional pictures of more clusters of people, Murray also captured on some of these negatives the seeming impropriety of traffic now reusing Elm Street for its intended mundane purpose, where only

minutes before at this same location American history had been drastically altered.

Seeing activity on the south side of Elm Street, Murray crossed over to the triangle of land between Elm and Main Streets. Taking a shot towards the grassy knoll and concrete pergola area, Murray at about this time probably used his second camera for the first time. Loaded with the same 36-exposure Plus-X type black-and-white film as his first camera, this second camera was mounted with either his 85mm or 105mm telephoto lens. Murray took a frame looking toward the triple underpass, upon which can be seen a few spectators, and then he shot an additional view of the crowd at the base of the knoll.

Murray next directed his attention to activity near a round metal "City of Dallas" storm sewer cover at the south curb of Elm Street. Crouching down slightly, Murray photographed officer J. D. Foster.

A telephoto view of the north, knoll side of Elm St. At left Deputy Sheriff Walthers begins to cross the street.

Nine minutes after the shooting, officer J. D. Foster points in the direction of the Book Depository building.

The officer was pointing in the general direction of the Book Depository, the front of which can be seen in the background. A Hertz advertisement sign on the building's roof includes a lighted time-and-temperature indicator which reads "12:39."

Deputy Sheriff Eddy Raymond "Buddy" Walthers is looking toward where Foster is pointing, while a man with a light jacket and plaid shirt, who does not appear from his dress to be a law officer, peers toward the camera lens. This civilian may be a spectator who held up some type of sign during the motorcade, and who can be seen in the Abraham Zapruder amateur movie film and a photo taken by UPI photographer Frank Cancellare, close to this present location.

Nine minutes ago, upon hearing gunshots, Walthers had run to the railroad yard from his position at the corner of Houston and Main Streets. Just moments ago he had crossed to this location, "... looking at the grass to see if some shots had been fired and some of them might had chugged into this turf here and it would give an indication ... if they were shots and not just blanks or something. ..."[7]

Officer Foster had been stationed on top of the triple underpass. Witnessing the shooting, he believed the shots to have come from the vicinity up around Elm and Houston Streets, and he had moved "... down the roadway there, down to see if I could find where any of the shots hit."[8]

Between 12:39 and 12:40 Murray took a series of seven photos of the activity here [roll 1, #13-19], including Walthers lighting a cigarette, and then stooping over and feeling in the grass. Another man with sandy hair and dressed in a suit is also seen in two frames bending over and probing the area with his left hand. Later, critics of the Warren Commission claimed that a spent bullet had been recovered at this time, citing the interpretation of photographic blow-ups of these Murray prints, as well as a similar series of photos made about the same time by *Dallas Times Herald* photographer William Allen. An article in the

Contact prints of four of Murray's photos of the sewer cover sequence.

A man in a suit probes the ground while Walthers and Foster look on.

December 1963 *New Republic* by Richard Dudman also reported that a police inspector had told Dudman that upon entering the area at the side of the street where the President had been shot, they had ". . . found another bullet in the grass."[9]

In his later testimony before a lawyer representing the Warren Commission, Officer Foster stated that they "found where one shot had hit the turf there at the location." He indicated that the bullet hit the turf at the concrete corner of the manhole cover and ricocheted out. Years later when asked by a researcher if he had observed the plainclothesman at the scene, ". . . picking up a bullet and putting it in his pocket or anything like that," Foster replied, "No sir."[10]

The similarities between the Murray and Allen photographic sequences have caused some confusion among researchers as to whose photos are whose. Many researchers have treated the two sequences as made by the same person. The Murray and Allen photographs indicate interest on the part of the officers at a spot about three feet to the west of the rectangular concrete frame surrounding the manhole.

An examination of first generation prints from the original Murray negatives show an area in the turf darker than the surrounding grass. When the question of a possible "slug in the grass" became a point touted by New Orleans District Attorney Jim Garrison during his investigation into the Kennedy assassination in 1967, Murray was curious enough to make blow-up prints from some of his negatives. The Murray photos showed no identifiable bullet.

When asked 22 years later about his thoughts as to what he was seeing while taking this group of photos, Murray stated, "At the time I was photographing, my honest opinion was that it looked like there had been heel marks, and something like a spiked heel had come out of the dirt and created a little mound of damp earth. I certainly didn't see any bullets or anything. The later speculation, and I'm willing to believe it, is that the mound was brain

matter from Kennedy's skull. It could well have been tissue. It was dark – muddy color – nothing to suggest brains or blood."

Detail of a photo by Willie Allen, made almost simultaneously with Murray photo 1-17.

Photographer William Allen recalled to this author in a 1987 interview, "It was my understanding that they were looking for either bullets or something like that, fragments of bullets or fragments of something. I didn't see them hold up a bullet and say, 'Hey, here's a bullet,' because I'm sure I would have photographed it if they picked up something like that. . . . I know I would have photographed it if they picked a bullet up. But I don't recall them picking up and holding anything up and saying, 'We got to keep this for evidence,' because I was standing right there with them the whole time."[11] The photos themselves are too inconclusive to be able to tell us what, if anything, was picked up off of the ground.

The unknown man dressed in a suit was identified in the 1990s by researcher Mark Oakes as Dallas FBI Agent Robert M. Barrett. Barrett was at the plaza during

Other civilians stand around the site near the sewer cover, as heavy traffic passes down Elm Street.

At 12:40 Murray shoots his last photo near the sewer cover. The man in the suit standing on the other side of the street looking toward the oncoming traffic has been identified by some researchers as Deputy Sheriff Roger Craig.

the early afternoon of November 22, 1963, and then is known to have been at the site of the police officer J. D. Tippit shooting and also assisting in the apprehension of suspect Lee Oswald at the Texas Theater. Barrett has stated in recent years that he is definitely not the man pictured in the Murray and Allen pictures. Some researchers have made an issue that in the last and only horizontal Murray view of this scene, this man appears to be putting something in his left pocket. Perhaps he did, though in the previous frame two civilians also have hands in their own pockets. Jim Garrison in his 1988 book *On the Trail of the Assassins* contended that Walthers "... is shown looking down at a bullet while a neatly dressed blond man is reaching down to pick it up. The unidentified blond man was wearing [a] plastic radio receiver clipped to his ear lobe." In Murray's clear, sharply focused photo, however, such an alleged receiver is completely invisible and clearly

not present! For the next several hours a police presence was always kept at this sewer cover site, and the Dallas Police Department took several photographs of this location.[12]

An ancillary use of the Murray and Allen photos was made by critics Richard Sprague and Gary Shaw, trying to correlate the testimony of Deputy Sheriff Roger Craig. The 27-year-old Craig had testified that following the gunshots, he had run down to this general area, and at around one o'clock, had observed a man running westerly down the grassy knoll. A Rambler station wagon, driven slowly, came parallel to the man, stopped, and the man jumped into the car. Later that day at police headquarters, Craig identified this running man as Lee Harvey Oswald.

Investigators chose not to believe Craig's account, while many critics of the government made Craig a darling of their cause, the implication in his testimony being that Oswald had help, and there was thus a conspiracy. Subsequently, Craig's relations with the sheriff's department soured and his credibility in this and other related matters suffered as he spoke out on various controversies dealing with the assassination. Fired as a deputy in 1967, Craig for a time was involved in the New Orleans District Attorney Jim Garrison investigation into the Kennedy assassination. After numerous personal problems and some self-perceived attempts upon his life, Craig shot himself to death in 1975.

Sprague and several others have identified a man they say to be Craig as seen in some of the Murray photographs. In both the Allen and Murray photo sequences, they have located a Rambler station wagon at 12:40 p.m. driving down Elm Street with a person whom they identify as Craig looking up Elm in that general direction.[13]

After taking the seven pictures near the sewer cover, Murray traveled to the southwest embankment of the triple underpass and made separate horizontal and vertical panoramic exposures of Elm, Main, and Commerce Streets, with the Texas School Book Depository, the Dal-Tex, and County Records buildings as the backdrop. The Hertz sign atop the Book Depository was on its temperature cycle displaying a mild 66 degrees Fahrenheit.[14]

About 20 minutes after the shooting, Murray, realizing the enormity of the event and the fact that he was at an important location with cameras, found a telephone and called Patsy Swank. Swank was a local part-time *LIFE* magazine "stringer" correspondent. She confirmed that Murray should consider himself on a photo assignment and told him also to be on the lookout for amateurs who had photographed the assassination.

By now activity within the Plaza was centering around the front entrance of the Book Depository. Murray walked up there and began making pictures. His first two pictures are vertical exposures of the Depository front entrance, showing a portion of all seven floors, including the

sixth floor corner window, which he later learned was the location where Lee Oswald was alleged to have fired his shots at the President.

Concerning his use of two cameras that day, Murray much later explained that he would use the telephoto lens only if he saw something that demanded a closer lens, but that in newsworthy situations like this, ". . . you probably rely on your wide-angle lens more." In his camera mounted with the wide-angle lens, he recorded two exposures of the crowd at the building's entrance, as well as a young black boy in the back seat of a police vehicle. The boy was 15-year-old Amos Lee Euins. At 12:36 Sergeant D. V. Harkness had located Euins near the Elm Street Extension by the railroad parking lot. Euins can be seen in this area in Murray's third photo (p. 82) taken when the photographer had been there earlier.

The boy told the sergeant that during the motorcade he had been at the corner of Houston and Elm Streets, and that the shots had come from the corner window under the Book Depository building's ledge. He later told investigators, "From where I was standing I could look across the street and see a large red brick building. . . . I heard a shot. I started looking around and then I looked up in the red brick building. I saw a man in a window with a gun and I saw him shoot twice. He then stepped back behind some boxes." According to Harkness, "After I took [Euins's] name and address and put this information on the radio, I then took him on the back of my three-wheel motorcycle and put him in inspector Sawyer's car." Inspector of Police J. Herbert Sawyer had arrived at the Depository front entrance shortly after 12:34. Following a quick perusal of the building, the inspector instructed officers not to allow anyone in or out. He then set up a command post near the entrance.[15]

One of Murray's photos of the Depository entrance allowed this author to help put to rest a minor controversy as regards another picture made that afternoon. Phillip L. Willis was a retired World War II major and executive automobile

A view toward the Book Depository and the north plaza area. An enlarged view of this scene shows that while interest continues at the sewer cover, across the street James Tague points out for Officer Foster the site near the underpass where he had been struck by something during the assassination.

Activity has shifted to the Book Depository building and Murray photographs its main entrance and facade.

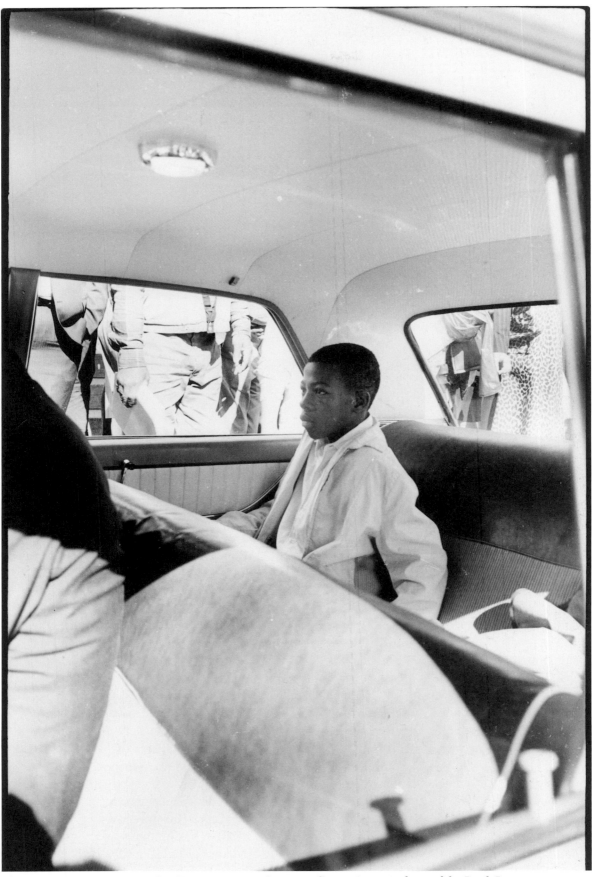

Assassination witness Amos Lee Euins is put into Inspector Sawyer's car in front of the Book-Depository.

Amateur photographer Phil Willis photographs the scene at the Book Depository front entrance before the civilians are pushed back from the area. Many people who later saw this picture thought the man at the extreme right wearing dark glasses was Jack Ruby.

salesman who lived in Dallas. He and his family had come to Dealey Plaza to view the motorcade. Willis had with him an Argus 35mm camera loaded with color slide film. Taking views before, during and after the assassination, Willis shot one view of the front of the Book Depository. This particular picture showed a crowd of citizens and police outside the building's main entrance a short time after the assassination. Noticed by Willis at a later date, as well as by various critics of the later government investigation, was a balding man in dark glasses. He is located at the far right of the 35mm transparency.

In November 1964, Willis was interviewed by a member of the Citizens Committee of Inquiry, which group was critical of the government's handling of the investigation. Willis showed the man the slide and commented that the figure appeared to be Jack Ruby, the man who shot and killed Lee Oswald Sunday morning at police headquarters. Willis remarked that the person in glasses looked so much like Ruby that it was "pitiful," and that when Willis later had a chance to see Ruby in person during the latter's trial in court, Willis believed the man in the picture looked just like Ruby. Willis also told the independent investigator that when FBI agents had previously questioned him, they had mentioned the man's presence in the photo before Willis did, and that they thought it was Ruby.[16] Though Ruby himself and several others testified that he was elsewhere during the time of the assassination, many critics clung to this photo as evidence of his being at the scene at least shortly after the shooting. This photo thus gave a conspiratorial feel to such a Ruby presence.

On first blush, the subject does look a bit like Ruby, especially with his receding hairline. Upon closer magnification of the picture, the subject, however,

Photo frame 1-27, taken by Jim Murray around the same time as the Willis slide on page 96, reveals the man in dark glasses as definitely not Jack Ruby.

Around 12:43 p.m. a police radio call instructs units to report Code 3 [emergency] to the corner of Elm and Houston Streets so that a controlled search of the Book Depository building could begin. Cycles and a squad car respond at the corner.

looks less bulky than Ruby and wears a shirt with no tie and an open collar. This author discovered within the photo record made by Jim Murray that afternoon two photographs taken at about 12:50 of the same Book Depository doorway as seen in the Willis slide with the Ruby look-alike present. One frame shows a police cruiser in the foreground, with a clear view of this same man on the other side of the cruiser. The Murray photo, however, positively shows that the man, when seen closer up and from a different angle, is not Ruby. Photographic evidence can at times be as misleading as it is informative. Though some uninformed or obstinate researchers may still cling to the Willis slide as indicating a Ruby presence, the discovery of the two Murray photos clearly lay to rest this speculation.[17]

Murray continued his photo coverage of the area. He made two shots looking east on Elm and Houston Streets showing a cruiser and motorcycles traveling down Houston to the Depository. KRLD television cameraman George "Sandy" Sanderson is also seen taking film of the street activity. Murray then walked up Houston where he made two additional shots, including a view showing most of the front of the Depository building. By this time the crowd in front of the Depository was being cleared out to the opposite side of Elm Street, and Murray finished his roll of 36 exposures taking shots of uniformed police, some holding shotguns, with the Depository sighted as an overpowering backdrop in his photographic composition.

Concurrently with his use of the first camera, Murray also was using his second camera mounted with the moderate telephoto lens. Among the cluster of photos Murray made, one can observe Howard Brennan in a series of three exposures shot of the front of the Book Depository. Following the shooting Brennan had told

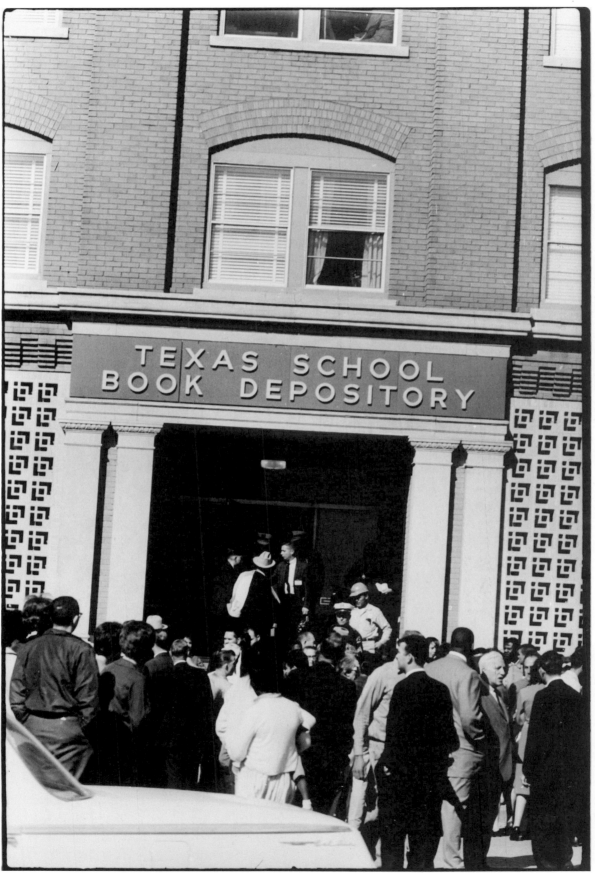

Howard Brennan, wearing a hard hat, stands at the entrance of the Texas School Book Depository near KTVT cameraman Don Cook who has a rectangular press identification badge pinned to his coat.

By 1:00 p.m. civilians have been pushed back from the front of the Book Depository building.

A heavy police presence is now on hand at the scene.

A police officer with a pump shotgun gazes up at the Texas School Book Depository building.

Jim Murray photographs Sheriff Bill Decker as he is interviewed outside the Book Depository building.

police officer Barnett what he had seen. He was brought to the front entrance but refused to enter the building and remained on the steps where he gave a description of the man he had seen in the window. He later related, ". . . I was confronted by a television reporter and cameraman. They wanted to interview me and find out what I knew about the shooting. I did not want to talk to him and I certainly did not want my picture broadcast. If there were more people involved than the young man I had seen, then showing me on television as an eyewitness would be like hanging a target over my heart for someone to shoot at. He kept asking 'Who are you, what do you know about the shooting of the President?' I turned my back on him without answering. He continued to try to get me to talk even though I moved away from him. Finally I said 'I don't know anything.' "[18]

Murray's photos show both cameraman Don Cook of KTVT and Walter Evans of KRLD radio on the steps near Brennan. Cook holds his camera and has a rectangular press identification badge on his coat lapel.

Two other pictures in this second camera sequence include views of Dallas County Sheriff Bill Decker giving an interview while being filmed by WFAA-TV cameraman A. J. L'Hoste.

A. J. L'Hoste's camera view of Decker.

Shortly after 1:00 p.m., Dallas Police Sgt. Gerry Hill leans out of a sixth floor window, pointing to the corner window where an apparent sniper location and spent shell casings had been found moments earlier.

With the Dal-Tex building in the background, Murray photographs Dallas police officers on Houston Street.
Three of the officers hold shotguns as they all await developments.

Several of Jim Murray's pictures assist in putting to rest another of the so-called photographic controversies. Around 1:00 p.m. spectator Ernest Charles Mentesana filmed a short 8mm clip (photo at right) which portrayed police officers and men in civilian clothes in animated discussion on Houston Street across from the Book Depository building. A long gun is seen protruding from behind the circle of men.

A number of assassination critics have described this scene as one in which an assassin's weapon, in addition to the one found in the Depository building said to belong to Oswald, is being examined. Such a recovery of a second assassin's gun and subsequent hushing up of this fact would prove a conspiracy in the shooting of the President.

If there are two possible explanations to a question relating to the assassination – one simple and logical and the other complicated and incredible – some critics will typically be attracted to the latter explanation. Though some have worked themselves up to imagine scenarios for revealing the fact of this second assassin's gun, there is a simpler explanation. The weapon in question has neither a telescopic sight nor a sling, and the thick barrel protrudes seven or so inches past the stock. Comparing the Mentesana clip with an assortment of still photos made by Jim Murray and others, the film incidently portrays a Dallas police officer holding a pump shotgun, the butt of which is resting on his left hip and the barrel projecting in a 45° angle from his body. The weapon and its manner of being held compare obviously to other such photos, even to the end magazine cap seen on some of these shotguns. To any reasonable researcher, this sequence does not show a mysterious second rifle, but rather incidentally pictures a cop holding a police-issue shotgun.

Four Dallas police officers, one holding a shotgun, engage in conversation on Houston Street.

With his telephoto lens, Murray clicks off two frames showing Sergeant Gerald Hill yelling out of a sixth floor window at around 1:00 p.m. just after spent rifle shells had been located by officers inside, under the corner window to which he is pointing. Four more pictures are made of a group of cops poised with shotguns and located at the Houston and Elm intersection.

His first 36-exposure roll of Plus-X film used-up, Murray inserted a fresh 20-exposure roll into his first camera with the wide-angle lens, and took four more exposures of activities around Houston and Elm Streets. Frames #4 & #5 show cops on the east side of Houston Street beginning to set up a rope line to keep spectators back. At about 12:54 p.m. a broadcast had gone over police radio channel 2 requesting a Fire Department Rescue Unit to respond with rope, the paneled vehicle arriving on location shortly thereafter.

Sometime after 1:00 p.m., while making the phone call to Swank, Murray had apparently missed the arrest near the Elm and Houston corner of a strange acting and seemingly intoxicated man named Larry Florer. Murray now went into the sheriff's office and recorded with both his cameras Florer seated in the office. Assassination eyewitnesses also there and seen in some of Murray's photos include the John Chism family, Charles Brehm and Hugh Betzner.

Amateur photographer Mary Moorman.

While in the sheriff's office, Murray made contact with Mary Moorman, an amateur photographer who was at the shooting scene. Moorman had taken an important Polaroid picture at the time the President was shot in the head. Murray tried to get the picture committed for *LIFE* magazine, but it was already secured by UPI. Murray took a picture of Moorman in the County Press Room, while the young woman was using a phone.

As Murray passed a bar close to Dealey Plaza, he took a photo of the interior. This blow-up shows the bar's television tuned to CBS news anchor Walter Cronkite who is reporting on the assassination which took place only yards away from where the bar patrons are sitting. At about this time Cronkite is in the process of announcing the President's death.

Murray was now fast running out of film, and would be in trouble if something important broke. Reluctantly, he decided it better to leave for a short time to get more film, rather than be caught on the spot without a means of recording possible important activity. Thus, at about 1:15 Murray walked back down Houston to Elm Street, shooting off several frames with both cameras. Two frames include cops on Houston with the Dal-Tex building in the background. Chalked on the building wall is a graffiti message reading, "If you want to live longer stay off the highways."

Murray records his taxi driver's reaction to the news of the shooting.

Murray caught a passing taxi and went down to the Elko Camera store at Main and Akard Streets. The cab driver had not heard about the shooting; and as Murray told him the news, the driver turned around and Murray made a reaction shot with his wide-angle lens. At Elko, Murray picked up a supply of black-and-white film,

switching to higher speed Tri-X, with an ASA of 400, rather than the ASA rating of 125 of the Plus-X film. This would give him more flexibility for shooting interiors.

Returning to the sheriff's office some time after 1:30 p.m., Murray finished up his two rolls in the cameras with additional shots of the office with witnesses and others sitting around waiting to have their statements recorded. Reloading with fresh Tri-X film, Murray then left the building for the corner of Elm and Houston, where with his telephoto lens he made three exposures of Elm Street in the direction of the underpass. Shortly after returning to the Plaza, Murray ran into Duane Robinson, a photographer friend who worked out of the Kincaid Photo Studio Service on Routh Street, a local gathering place for professional photographers. Murray gave Robinson his first two rolls of film, as well as his recent third roll on which there were only 14 exposures, Murray pulling it from the

Back at the sheriff's office Murray takes a photo through a glazed door of various assassination witnesses, including the John Chism family of three sitting on the couch, and of Larry Florer who is wearing glasses and sitting in an arm chair near the center of this picture.

camera early to expedite processing. Robinson brought the three rolls to Kincaid's to be quickly processed and then to have contact prints made of each roll.[19]

Now becoming aware that the assassin's position had been supposedly discovered in an upper-story corner window of the Texas School Book Depository building, Murray took two pictures of the front west end of the building using his telephoto lens. These he followed with five additional exposures of activity on the street level, and then eight pictures of the upper front east side of the building. In the photos showing the sixth floor corner window, activity is evident within. A member of the Crime Scene Section of the police department, most probably R. L. Studebaker, can be observed through the window as he examines this area.

Murray then ". . . roamed around the fringes of Dealey Plaza looking for amateur photos and shooting a few myself." The shocking announcement of the death of the President had been made around 1:30 p.m. Murray, though still somewhat dazed by the events, decided that he should begin to round out his photo take with other locations. He had pretty much covered all that could be shot at this location, and could not get into the Depository building itself. Before leaving the Plaza he took a few panoramic shots from an upper window of the Terminal Annex Post Office on Houston Street, which overlooks the entire Plaza area from the south. All told, Murray had taken just under 100 exposures at Dealey Plaza between approximately 12:33 and 3:30 p.m.

Murray hitched a ride to Parkland Memorial Hospital with another newsman and clicked-off four exposures there. The only activity at the hospital was in a makeshift press area in a hospital classroom that was set up for reports on the condition of Governor Connally, who had been shot along with the President. Murray then went over to the Dallas Trade Mart where the President was to have spoken. He took a series of shots of the deserted dining room. The head table with fruit cups, salads, rolls, pie and china was now set up for no one. A few workmen were slowly removing the dinnerware and breaking down the tables.

At some point during the afternoon, Murray took a series of exposures at the County Press Room of a handbill which had been circulated on Dallas streets on Wednesday and Thursday. The flyer was made to look like a criminal reward poster including a profile and front face picture of President Kennedy with the heading: "Wanted For Treason." Inflammatory charges were listed under the photographs. It was later learned that several thousand of these handbills had been printed up at the behest of a right wing associate of former General Edwin Walker. The bad taste of the flyer was now magnified by the President's murder in the streets of Dallas.

The afternoon was pretty much a blur. Like most everyone, I was in a state of shock. Operating independently as a free-lancer, I didn't have the news organization backup to keep me pointed everywhere the events were breaking. I had left my car downtown and hopped rides with other photographers and newsmen. One stop was at the KRLD-TV newsroom. The enormity of the Kennedy murder was sinking in. One veteran newsman was crying as he sorted through the chaotic reports coming in.

In the late afternoon Murray finally returned to Dealey Plaza to pick up his car. An incident involving Murray's car gave the photographer an insight into the reliability of eyewitnesses. According to Murray, this minor incident is typical of the kind of "misinformation" that has a way of attaching itself to the assassination events.

"When I returned to my car parked next to the School Book Depository, it was blocked in by police motorcycles. As I started to get in the car, a uniformed officer approached and asked if I was 'James Murray from San

Amid boxes of books, a Dallas Police Department crime scene investigator examines the sixth floor corner window area for evidence in the shooting.

A panorama of the north side of Dealey Plaza including the Book Depository building and "grassy knoll."

The Parkland Hospital classroom from where press announcements regarding the gunshot victims were made.

The head table at the Trade Mart, where the President was to have delivered his Dallas speech.

A right-wing handbill distributed in Dallas prior to the Friday motorcade.

Antonio?' " TV newsmen had a certain quasi-celebrity status among Dallas lawmen, and when the officer asked the question, Murray was a bit flattered that the cop apparently recognized him from past contacts – and even remembered that he had moved to San Antonio. He was quickly disabused of that notion, however.

"The officer told me that a witness in the building across the street reported that shortly after the assassination someone had come off the Depository loading dock, ran to this car and 'put something in the trunk.'" The police had obtained Murray's name and address through a license check with state records in Austin. Since the address was not local, the car had remained beside the Depository all afternoon, and the witnesses report sounded suspicious, the police wanted to see who would appear.

Murray had indeed run to the car from the sheriff's office to get his cameras from the trunk following the shooting, and sometime later had also climbed up and jumped down from the loading dock, looking for scenes to photograph. But his action had not been as ominous as the unnamed "witness" had described.

Murray was aware that sometime that afternoon a police officer had been killed, but he did not slow down his activity enough to learn that the alleged killer had been captured or that the prisoner was also the chief suspect in the Kennedy assassination. As far as Murray knew, the police were still hunting for killers. With that sobering realization in mind, Murray wanted to make darn sure that the officer satisfied himself as to the trunk's content. He offered his keys to the officer, who replied he would rather Murray open it himself. The officer then searched the trunk's contents as well as the back seat where a large Auricon sound camera case was located. Murray insisted the officer carefully check out the camera case to his full satisfaction. The cop then said that the "chief" wanted to talk to Murray, and "gently but firmly" led

Murray by the arm to Deputy Chief George Lumpkin, who was situated near the Depository entrance. The matter was quickly straightened out, though it gave Murray his first taste of how eyewitnesses can mix up recollections during stressful events.[20]

I went back to my car and then on to Kincaid's. My first three rolls had been processed and contacted. I put my name on them and gave them, plus the next three unprocessed rolls to Shel Hershorn who was gathering stuff for shipment to *LIFE*. Shel was a Dallas free-lancer who did a lot of *LIFE* work through Black Star. He got back to Dallas from an out-of-town assignment late in the day. Normally, film shot for *LIFE* goes to the New York editorial offices, but that day, with the magazine on deadline, Kennedy film was being sent directly to Chicago, where the magazine was printed.

By evening *LIFE* had set up headquarters at the Adolphus Hotel. Murray checked in there for a possible assignment and was sent back to Parkland Hospital to see if anything was new concerning the condition of Governor Connally. It was now dark, sunset occurring at 5:22 p.m. Murray was unable to get access into the hospital. He made do shooting several frames with both his cameras loaded with fresh film. He photographed the looming hospital facade with all its lights ablaze. Murray's next destination was the Police Department in the Dallas City Hall, where he had learned that the captured assassination suspect was being held.

The crush of newsmen outside the Homicide office was a madhouse – like a feeding frenzy. By evening the national and foreign press had arrived. Oswald was being held on the [fifth] floor, and Homicide was on the third floor. He would be taken back and forth through this incredible mass of photographers. We all just waited there in just this packed little sardine-like group. There was a photographer from the [New York] *Daily News* that was an asthmatic, and he had come down there with a Hasselblad with a sports finder. It was the only thing he had. He had been covering some sports event, and they said 'get on a plane and get to Dallas.' We were packed in so tightly that he was having an asthma attack, and he couldn't even fall out. It was just ghastly.[21]

Murray is now not exactly sure just when he arrived at the 7-foot-wide, third floor corridor which served the Homicide office. He believes his arrival was between 7 and 8 o'clock in the evening. A careful examination of the two rolls of film he shot with his two cameras help reconstitute a chronology of his activity. His swapping of lenses between his two cameras to give him a shooting camera with a wide-angle lens attached for a better view in a tight space situation, complicates the reconstituting of the events. The first activity he records at headquarters is of Oswald being brought down the corridor and then into the Homicide office which was marked "317" on the door. Though he did manage several views of Oswald, he knew they would print up as less than perfect, exhibiting the jostling of bodies in the corridor.

Murray recalls one photographer, Lawrence J. Schiller, a 27-year-old photojournalist who did work for *Paris Match* and *LIFE*. Schiller had a reputation as one who would do almost anything for a story and a good photo. In the crush of the moment Schiller had elbowed Murray out of a good shooting position. Murray was not pleased and resolved that if the occasion presented itself, next time he would make sure to get a good shot of the accused assassin.[22]

At around 7:10 p.m. Oswald had been arraigned by Judge David L. Johnston, justice of the peace for the second precinct of Dallas County, for the murder of Officer J. D. Tippit. This was the police officer who had been gunned down earlier that afternoon, not too long before and not too far from the place of Oswald's arrest in the Texas Theater. According to police records, Oswald was brought to a third "show-up" lineup for witness identifications around 7:50 p.m., and had also made a phone call and been visited by a representative of the Dallas Bar Association.

Once he had a position in the corridor in front of the glazed door with lettering on the glass reading, "HOMICIDE AND ROBBERY BUREAU," Murray steadfastly kept his good spot. This location afforded Murray an opportunity to see into the office and photograph through the glazing any unusual activity occurring there. In the back right side of the room was a door which led to Homicide Captain Will Fritz's inner office, where Oswald was being interviewed and examined.

In one of Murray's early, through-the-glass-door photos, Justice of the Peace Johnston is observed standing while FBI agent James P. Hosty, Jr., talks with another man, who appears to be Assistant District Attorney Bill Alexander. Hosty was the case officer for Oswald in Dallas. Though he had never met Oswald, the agent had visited the place where Oswald's wife, Marina, was living, and had spoken with her briefly. Just prior to November 22, Oswald had written and dropped off a note for Hosty at the FBI office. According to Hosty, this note told him not to bother his wife but to talk directly to the writer. Yet the note was unsigned! By the end of this weekend, Hosty would be ordered by his superior to destroy the note, and its exact content and possible threatening tone would never be known for sure. Upon Oswald's arrest on Friday, Hosty went to participate in the interrogation, and Oswald became agitated by his presence. According to Hosty's account, the agent remained at police headquarters until after 7:00 p.m., when he left and had dinner.[23]

Shooting through the Homicide Bureau's glazed door, Murray photographs FBI agent Jim Hosty, Jr., conferring with Assistant DA Bill Alexander. Hosty is holding a Dallas Times Herald *evening newspaper with a headline reading, "President Dead, Connally shot." Judge David Johnston, wearing glasses, looks in Murray's direction.*

Whenever he saw activity, Murray took a photo or two, even if he had no idea if it was significant. Nineteen-year-old Buell Wesley Frazier, an Oswald co-worker who had driven him to work that Friday morning, was for a time under suspicion himself. In several frames made by Murray it appears that he captured Frazier, his sister, Linnie Mae Randall, and their Baptist minister, Rev. Campble, leaving the Homicide office sometime around 9:00 p.m.

Using both cameras, Murray had also photographed two motorcycle policemen a bit earlier. Both officers had participated in the noontime motorcade. He made one frame of Hollis B. McLain, and took five wide-angle shots of Officer James M. Chaney as he was being questioned by the press near the Homicide office. He also took six telephoto shots, four of Chaney's head and helmet and two

reference photos showing his breast nametag so as to remember his name.

At about this time Bill Lord of ABC News did a brief interview of Chaney, recording his activities for broadcast over WFAA television. Chaney recalled of the motorcade incident:

I was riding on the right rear fender. We had proceeded west on Elm Street at approximately 15 to 20 miles an hour. We heard the first shot. I thought it was a motorcycle backfiring and, uh, I looked back over to my left and also President Kennedy looked back over his left shoulder. Then the, uh, second shot came, well then I looked back just in time to see the President struck in the face by the second bullet. He slumped forward into Mrs. Kennedy's lap, and uh, it was apparent

On the fifth floor corridor, motorcycle officer James M. Chaney is interviewed about the assassination.

Detective W. E. Barnes holds prints he had just made of Lee Oswald's hands.

Chief Curry, Captain Fritz, DA Wade and Judge Johnston prepare to allow the press to see Oswald.

to me that we're being fired upon. I went ahead of the President's car to inform Chief Curry that the President had been hit. And then he instructed us over the air to take him to Parkland Hospital, and he had Parkland standing by. I went on up ahead of the – to notify the officer that was leading the escort that he had been hit and we're going to have to move out. [The shot,] it was back over my right shoulder.[24]

According to police records, Oswald was in the homicide office at 9:00 p.m. when paraffin casts were made of his right face and two hands, followed by prints being taken of both hands by Detectives J. B. "Johnny" Hicks and Sergeant William E. "Pete" Barnes. In the paraffin cast procedure, warm wax is painted over the skin of the subject followed by gauze and more paraffin. The resulting cast is removed and tested to reveal traces of powder residue which can adhere to the skin following the firing of a weapon. Murray recorded with both his cameras the police technicians leaving the homicide room after the casts and prints had been made. In one sequence one man carries a pot and a paintbrush, while his companion holds several bulky manila files similar to those reported to have contained the paraffin casts. On the other camera film strip, Barnes is seen holding a container, a roller, and a sheet of paper showing a full right hand print with possibly another print sheet under that. Later results indicated that there was nitrate on both casts of Oswald's hands, though no nitrates were present on the right face and cheek cast.[25]

Apparently ceding to the reporters and photographers clamoring for news, a rolled-up shirtsleeved man comes through the Homicide doorway and holds up what appears to be a fingerprint card exhibiting Oswald's ten prints. Murray shoots the scene from behind the man. The print card is held up while a horde of news and cameramen press forward to see and film

it, including Larry Schiller in the front row wearing a short-sleeved shirt.

Murray recalls, "As we pushed and jockeyed for position in the hall outside the Homicide office, newsmen were clamoring for a chance to question Oswald and to get a better look at him than they had been getting as he was hustled to and from his cell."

Nearing midnight there was activity in the Homicide office. Dallas District Attorney Henry Wade, Police Chief Jesse Curry, Justice of the Peace Johnston and Homicide Captain Will Fritz are seen conferring in the crowded room. Then Curry, followed by Wade, steps out to address the press. Murray relates, "I was standing next to Police Chief Jesse Curry and District Attorney Henry Wade outside the Homicide office that Friday night. From overhearing their conversation, it was evident they were caving in to media pressure by bringing Oswald down to the basement 'press conference.' They were anxious to show that Oswald wasn't being mistreated. They forgot security concerns."[26]

It had been decided to show Oswald to the press while allowing no one to ask questions of him. Wade briefed the press before Oswald was led out. Murray had never competed head-to-head with the world press on a huge story. He was accustomed to certain ground rules, but that night it was dog-eat-dog. Jammed against Murray's right side was Schiller.

It soon became obvious that if a photo opportunity occurred, I might be bowled over and get pictures of nothing but Schiller's elbows. I was determined not to let that happen. I had a better view into the homocide office than others in the hall. When Oswald was brought out, I saw him a fraction of a second before the others. I leaned into Schiller and held my ground until I made two shots. One caught Oswald with Curry and a white-hatted detective beside him. I shot again as the press screamed

Murray snags a full front view of Oswald as the prisoner leaves the Homicide Bureau.

Oswald reacts to a reporter's question and microphone thrust at him.

questions and a microphone was thrust into Oswald's face.[27]

The ground rules laid out on the third floor were doomed from the start. By the time Oswald was brought into the basement show-up room, all the space there was packed by press and officials and at least one unauthorized visitor, Jack Ruby, who had managed to bluff his way in looking like he belonged there. Questions were flung towards Oswald, and following his giving a few brief comments, he was pulled out of the room when it became clear that no one was playing by the civil rules as established by the Dallas top cop.

With his location on the third floor, Murray did not have the time to get to the basement room, though he did reach the basement in time to position himself to make several hasty views of the clogged corridor and the front of the show-up room itself. A careful inspection of these Murray pictures reveals just a peek of the head of Oswald, the prisoner surrounded by police officers.

My perch was on a row of cabinets paralleling the hall on its left side near its north end. Knowing the line-up room was jammed and offered little chance for a clear shot, I chose the line of cabinets for an unobstructed view of Oswald when he came out. I shot a picture as he and his escort came under me. He was ringed by detectives with these typical western hats that Texas lawmen favor. Oswald looked up with a sort of sullen and quizzical look, as if to say: 'What the hell are you doing up there?'[28]

This is undoubtedly the best known of Murray's pictures taken that day. *LIFE* magazine published it on page 38 of their November 29, 1963, issue with an incorrect caption reading "Ninety minutes after President was shot, detectives wearing ten-gallon hats hustle Oswald into Dallas Police Headquarters 'I didn't kill anybody,'

Murray's basement corridor sequence showing Oswald being led past him.

"Portrait of the Assassin"

Murray manages to photograph Oswald near the jail entrance.

he insists." An extreme blow-up of Oswald's face, copied directly from the image on the page in *LIFE* magazine, was used on the dust jacket and paperback cover of the book, *Portrait of the Assassin*, first published in 1965. This pro-Commission volume was written by one of its members, Gerald R. Ford, then a member in the United States House of Representatives, and the future President of the United States.[29]

Following the short, near bedlam-like experience of Oswald being shown to the press, the accused murderer was whisked down the corridor to the jail elevator taking him to the upper floors of the building. Murray was out of film in one camera and had one frame left in the other. Hoping for a final shot of Oswald, he avoided the press stampede and took a public elevator to the fourth floor. The elevator door opened at the jail reception area. On this floor was located the department's Identification Bureau. Just on the

other side of the office grillwork, Murray spied Oswald surrounded by several officers. It looked like he was being checked in. To the left of Oswald was Assistant Jailer Tommy V. Todd. Murray managed to use up his last frame photographing the prisoner on the other side of the grill.[30]

According to jail records, Oswald was again fingerprinted and official police photographs were taken of him. By 1:10 a.m. the prisoner was brought up to his cell on the fifth floor and then at 1:30 brought down again to the ID Bureau for arraignment before Justice of the Peace Johnston on the charge of killing the President. Following this non-public arraignment, Oswald was brought back to his cell remaining there until morning light on November 23.

Leaving the police station sometime after 12:30 a.m. that Saturday morning, Murray dropped off his film. He found himself driving around aimlessly, listening to radio reports. "For the first time that day,

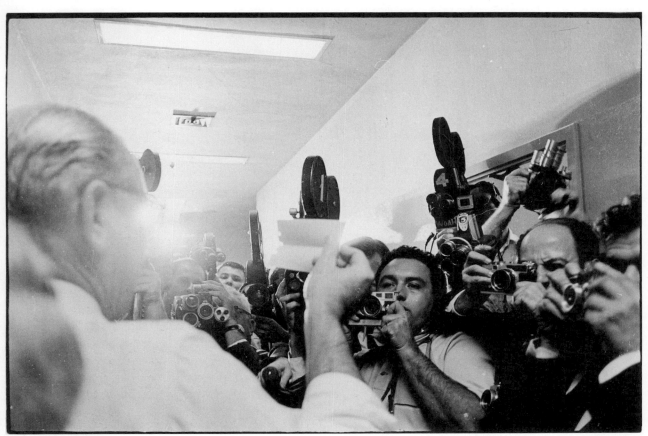

A graphic example of the crush of newsmen at the Dallas Police Headquarters. Here photographers shoot a card containing Oswald's fingerprints. The cameraman in front wearing a light, short-sleeved shirt is Larry Schiller.

I had nothing to do, and I finally shed my first tears. I stopped at a friend's house. All of the people gathered knew that Kennedy's death had changed our city and the whole world. But I don't think any of us realized how profoundly it would change things."

Those who watched the activities at the Dallas police headquarters via the frequent television reports of that weekend can vividly remember the crush of activity and seeming circus side-show atmosphere which was later almost universally condemned. Murray, a local observer and critic of the Dallas scene, gives some insight into the factors that brought this about:

The city has taken lots of lumps for the lax security. Having been very critical of the Dallas political scene in the 50s and early 60s, I now find myself in the odd position of defending Dallas against critics who

haven't always made the distinction between sinister motives and just plain stupidity. When the roof fell in, Dallas authorities were simply unprepared to deal with the enormity of it.

You had to have been a newsman in Dallas in the pre-assassination years to understand how the authorities perceived the media. I daresay it was different from any U.S. city – at least those cities with a "watch dog" press.

There was a cozy, basically unhealthy relationship between ownership of the papers and the municipal government. They were members of the same "club." The authorities had no reason to keep the press at arm's length, because they knew that negative stories, dug up by street reporters, seldom found their way into the papers. Consequently, they were conditioned to let the press have its way – even when it came to protecting a suspected presidential assassin. Aside from fighting off other newsmen, my access to Oswald was never challenged at the city jail.

This "kid gloves" treatment of the press was a critical factor in what occurred after the Kennedy assassination. In effect the authorities let the news organizations set the ground rules for coverage of Oswald.

I believe to this day, that misjudgments in handling the press – and not a "plot" – were responsible for Oswald's murder. It's not surprising that a "hanger-on" like [Jack] Ruby could get in the Police Station. The basement should have been sealed off from everyone – including the media. We would have howled, but Oswald would have lived to stand trial. And when he was killed it was much more damaging to the

national psyche than the death of a president.[31]

Murray was also a witness to part of the story relating to the day of the death of Oswald. Sunday morning, November 24, was the designated time for the transfer of Lee Oswald from the City Police Headquarters down to the more secure County Jail on Houston Street. Murray was given an assignment by *LIFE* representatives in Dallas to go to the sheriff's office and photographically cover the arrival of the prisoner. Unable to gain access into the Houston Street building, Murray took up a position near the jail's auto entrance. There was a throng of other press as well as hundreds of spectators lining the street. Sheriff Bill Decker was also on the sidewalk talking with members of his department and the news media.

Sometime around 11:25 a.m. an ambulance rushed by headed west on Main Street. Recalls Murray, "We didn't connect it to Oswald until there was a flurry around

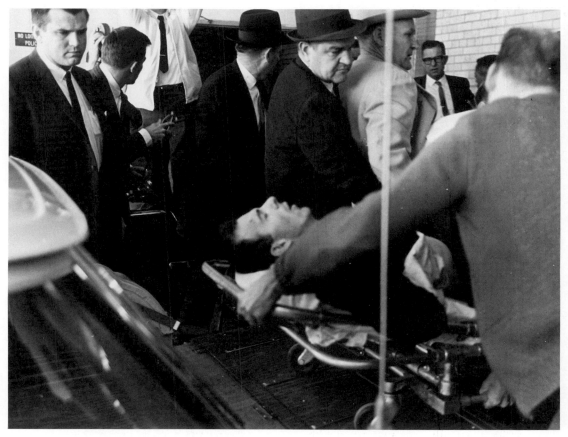

A mortally wounded Oswald arrives at Parkland Hospital on Sunday, November 24.

Decker. I asked him what was going on and he said something like, 'Somebody got to Oswald.' " At about 11:17 a.m. in the basement of the police station, as Oswald was being escorted by officers through a gauntlet of press observers, Jack Ruby had lunged at Oswald firing a single point blank shot into the prisoner's abdomen. Within several minutes the unresponsive, ashen-faced Oswald was shoved into an ambulance and rushed off to Parkland Hospital.

Once it was realized that Oswald was on his way to the hospital, Murray knew that's where he wanted to be. His car was several long blocks away. Walking out into the traffic of Main Street, the photographer hailed a passing automobile occupied by two women on their way to the Carolinas. Murray persuaded them to turn the car around and drive him to the hospital some three miles away.

Oswald had arrived at the hospital at about 11:32 a.m. and was gurneyed into Trauma Room 2 in the emergency area of the hospital. Murray soon found himself one of many press also at the hospital. Though he could not see into the area where Oswald was being treated, he could look through a window and thought to photograph a general scene. Hospital aid Era Lumpkin later recounted to investigators that "cameramen were at the window on the door behind the Admitting Clerk's, trying to take pictures. I took a piece of paper and taped it to the glass."

Frustrated by not having anything to shoot, Murray figured that Oswald would probably be taken from the ground floor emergency area up to the surgery area on the second floor. "I knew my way around Parkland. I went up to the first floor hoping to get on an elevator to two. I punched the "Up" button and about the same time heard the commotion of the elevator being loaded on the floor below."

Oswald's condition was critical. The bullet which penetrated his body had hit every major organ in its flight path. The many physicians who had rushed for the call were directed by Dr. M. T. "Pepper" Jenkins. An endotrachael tube was inserted,

three venous cutdowns were made and he was given Ringer's lactate. Blood was quickly called for. It was soon determined to send Oswald up to emergency surgery.

Dr. Charles A. Crenshaw, a physician on the scene, wrote a controversial book in 1992 titled, *JFK: Conspiracy of Silence*, outlining his belief in a conspiracy to kill Kennedy. Crenshaw vividly recalled the elevator scene of getting the patient up to surgery. Comparing it to a "fire drill," Crenshaw described the dozen people pushing the gurney to the elevator, all the while minding the IV stand and anesthesia machine and squeezing into the elevator. Sally Lennon, an OB-GYN, held the door and operated the elevator. Several doctors including Jerry Gustafson pushed in, as did homicide Detective L. C. Graves. Graves had been on Oswald's left arm during the transfer and following the shooting had wrestled the gun from shooter Jack Ruby. According to Graves, ". . . and, so, we caught the elevator with him and with the doctors and nurses and went up to the second floor. . . ." But not before it stopped at the first floor. Crenshaw writes how the people on the first floor simply saw a mass of humanity as the elevator door opened, and had no idea that Oswald was aboard.

Murray was not sure what was coming up from the ground floor on the elevator, though just in case he had his camera ready. "The door opened on the first floor. The elevator was jammed with medicos and cops surrounding the gurney. There was yelling – probably some of it at my intrusion. My view was blocked, but I squeezed off a couple of quick shots before the door closed."[32]

Knowing he would not have an opportunity for any more Oswald pictures at the hospital, Murray tore back to the Adolphus Hotel where *LIFE* had established a temporary office. He was sent to Love Field where a courier was boarding a plane to take Murray's and other photographers' pictures on to Chicago where the magazine's regular issue was being torn apart and remade for the assassination story.

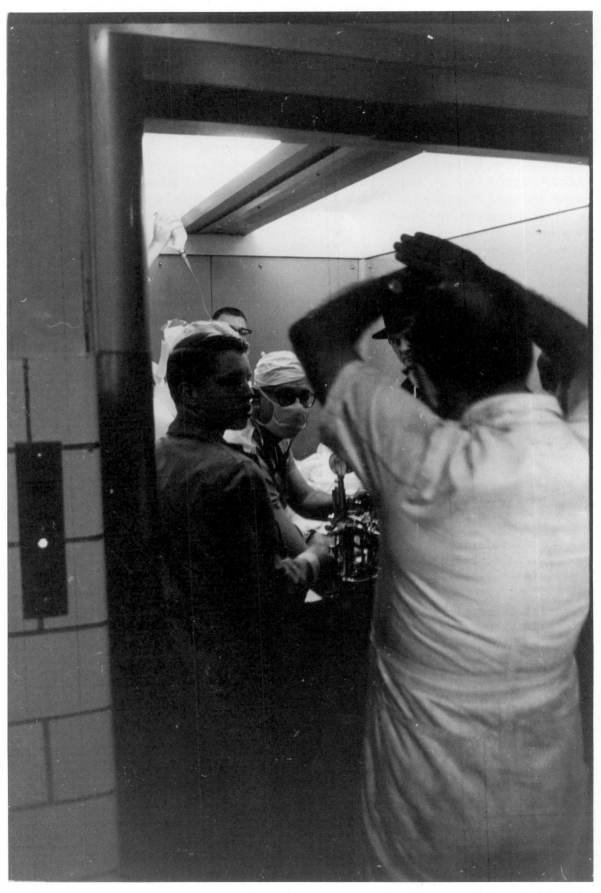

The elevator in which Oswald was being brought up for emergency surgery opens to reveal a crush of medical staff, including Dr. Jerry Gustafson, as well as police detective L. C. Graves, wearing a hat.

Later in the day Murray accompanied *LIFE* writer Tommy Thompson hunting for material on the new assassin, Jack Ruby. They found Ruby's Oak Cliff apartment and Murray made some pictures of it.[33]

Shortly before or after the assassination weekend, (Murray is not sure of the time frame) the photographer took a series of eight pictures of an outdoor Dallas billboard. He thought the sign was a good example of the "extreme local political temper" exhibited by a segment of the Dallas community. The billboard was located near the north central expressway around Hall Street. Flanked by illustrations of the Texas state and United States flags were large capital letters which read, "BE A SUPER PATRIOT!" Under that admonition was the request, "Help Impeach EARL WARREN," followed by three smaller lines, "For information write to Committee to Impeach Earl Warren, Box 1757, Dallas. A PAID POLITICAL ADVERTISEMENT." To the political right wing, including the John Birch Society and other such groups, the Chief Justice of the United States was one of the most notorious enemies of their cause, as the so-called liberal Warren Court's decisions were contrary to the right wing's patriotic ideals and goals.

The Murray shot of this billboard was taken at 11:25 one morning looking southwest towards the Dallas business district. The high-rise Southland Life building and the Sheraton Dallas Hotel on Olive Street are prominent backdrop buildings, while in the distance, as seen through the billboard's support structure, is the White Plaza Hotel. It turned out Jim Murray wasn't the only one to photograph this billboard and its vitriolic content. It came out many months later during the investigation into Jack Ruby's whereabouts during the assassination weekend, that Ruby also had an interest in this sign. The day of the assassination Ruby had apparently been upset by a full page paid advertisement appearing in the *Dallas Morning News* attacking President Kennedy and signed by an "Abe Weissman." Ruby was of Jewish lineage, and it seemed to him that the use of this Jewish name in such a classless and incendiary political advertisement attacking the President reflected badly on Jews who were in a distinct minority in "Big D." The address given in the ad was P.O. Box 1792.

The Friday night of the assassination found Ruby around midnight at police headquarters where he was present when Oswald was brought into the showup room to be seen by the press. After several forays into the night, in the very early morning of Saturday, November 23, Ruby woke up his apartment roommate, George Senator and Curtis "Larry" Crawford, a handymam from Ruby's Carousel strip club. He made them go with him to look at this impeachment sign. Ruby had Crawford bring a Polaroid camera with flash bulbs, and take three photos of the sign. According to both Senator and Crawford, Ruby was incensed by the billboard. He told Senator he did not understand how anyone would have the nerve to put up such a sign, and they would have to be "Commies" or "Birchers."

At a waffle shop, over coffee, Ruby continued to spew forth about the billboard, finding the similarity of post office box numbers on the sign and in the Weissman ad to be significant. Around 6:20 a.m., after dropping Crawford off, Ruby and Senator went to the post office to attempt unsuccessfully to find out who owned the box numbers. Just what this bizarre incident was all about, or if it was just typical Ruby antics, as his friends seemed to believe, is unclear. Some have contended that Ruby didn't even know who Earl Warren was, but that the billboard's negative association was what made Ruby react to it. Murray's photo of the sign, taken without any knowledge of Ruby's interest in it, shows that the sign did do what it meant to do — attract attention.[34]

The "Impeach Earl Warren" sign, which was photographed by both Jim Murray and Jack Ruby.

On Monday, November 25, President Kennedy was laid to rest in solemn and magnificent ceremonies in Washington, D. C. The same day as the President's funeral two other principals in the assassination story were buried in Texas. At Fort Worth, Lee Oswald was quickly and somewhat pathetically buried, having been borne to his grave by newsmen. The witnesses to the ceremonies were his immediate family of five, police, Secret Service agents, press and several curious civilians. That same day in Dallas, the funeral of police officer J. D. Tippit, slain by Oswald, took place. The officer was laid to rest in the section of Laurel Land Memorial Cemetery newly dedicated for honored city dead. Hundreds of mourners, including scores of his fellow officers, were there as was his grieving widow, son, daughter and relatives.

Jim Murray had been assigned to cover the Tippit funeral. One of his photos captured the immense emotions of the event. It pictured Mrs. Tippit sobbing at graveside while being comforted by officer Bill Anglin and flanked by her brothers and children. The December 6, 1963, issue of *LIFE* magazine reproduced the photo on two thirds of a page juxtaposed with a similar view of the Oswald family sitting at their gravesite. An article by Thomas Thompson graphically describing the two funerals was included above the photos. The article and two photos were also included in *LIFE*'s December "Memorial Edition."[35]

Following the weekend of November 22-25 and after the use of his photographs by *LIFE* magazine, Murray had his whole series of negatives sent to Black Star in New York. Black Star was a photo agency for use by authors, magazines, and the like, which sells reprint rights of its client photographers and gives sixty percent of the proceeds to the photographer. A number of Murray's pictures were used by European magazines. The photographer also continued to do some work on the subject of the assassination. An Italian magazine, *EPOCA*, a layout clone of *LIFE*, hired Murray to assist photographically in an anniversary issue. The photographer went around with an Italian reporter making pictures of Dallas people and scenes including Rev. Oscar Huber, the priest who had given the President the sacrament of Last Rites, and Marguerite Oswald, the accused assassin's loopy mother. Murray also did photographic work in covering part of the Jack Ruby murder trial.[36]

Murray became unhappy with how he saw some of his 1963 photos being used. In 1967 Josiah Thompson's book, *Six Seconds in Dallas: A Microstudy of the Kennedy Assassination,* was published. The book included legitimate purchases from Black Star photo agency of three of Murray's photos. The volume was regarded by most as a carefully researched work, unlike much of the other critical assassination literature being produced.[37]

Included in the Thompson book was a Murray photo enlargement replicated below an enlargement of a frame from an amateur film taken at the corner of Main and Houston Streets by Robert Hughes. The accompanying caption under the Murray photograph featuring the Depository windows indicated that it was taken "only moments" after the assassination, and showed boxes much lower in the window than the figure which was apparent in the Hughes film. Thompson's contention was that there was a figure in the Hughes frame visible in the window next to the supposed assassin's window, and that the figure had disappeared by the time Murray's picture was taken.[38] Murray says he was "appalled" by Thompson's interpretation of his photograph and told this writer:

The book says my photo was taken "only moments" after the assassination, and was taken "not far" from the Main and Houston intersection where the Hughes film was shot. Thompson was wrong on both counts, and careful research would have borne this out. My photo was taken at least ten minutes after the assassination, and from the intersection of Elm and Houston. This was a block closer to the Depository than Hughes's position. Therefore, my picture was made from a more acute upward angle than the Hughes film. Whatever "mysterious" object showed in the window in the Hughes film could not be seen in mine. In other words, my photo was misinterpreted to support an unproved theory.

And I thought that if a researcher who has academic credentials like Thompson had, could be so careless about finding out exactly when and from where a picture was taken, and jump to this conclusion that had no basis in fact, then I didn't have enough control over the photographs. You couldn't expect Black Star to get a pledge from everybody who used them that they weren't going to come to wild conclusions. In short, I took them back because I couldn't control their misuse. It's been very disturbing to me some of the fantasies that have arisen out of this – I don't know the answer, but I know that a lot of the conspiracy theories just don't hold water. I did not want my photographs to be misused to distort the facts and add to the controversy.[39]

Jim Murray took back possession of his original negatives, which for a period during the Jim Garrison investigation, he kept in a security box. Remaining in Dallas, Murray broadened his business to include work in film documentaries. Over the years he has been contacted by a few dozen Kennedy researchers. While admitting to a fascination of the subject of the assassination, Murray has found it bothersome to deal with many of the so-called researchers, and became selective about with whom he speaks. It was, therefore, a treat for this writer to have first met Murray in November 1985 and been invited late one night to Murray's office, filled with equipment, books, paraphernalia, and pictures. Located in an elderly commercial building only a few blocks from Dealey Plaza, the office gave one the feeling of an inner sanctum filled with comfortable clutter. Murray was careful and articulate when conversing about the assassination, not wanting his words to be misconstrued.

Murray strikes one as having thought about the 1963 events and its aftermath not only from the narrow viewpoint of a witness to some of those events, but as one trying to understand the event's full impact. He is a photographer of the events who speaks about the assassination photographs with a critical eye. Concerning the critics who have used photographs to aid their theories, Murray comments: "You can read just about anything you want to in a photograph. I have never found anything in any of my photographs that supports any of the conspiracy theories that I have heard. . . . I have shown prints to people who have pored over them with magnifying glasses, and have found everybody but the risen Elvis lurking in the shadows."

Murray remained active with a myriad of film projects including a major film documentary about sculptor Henry Moore. In 1989 Jim was felled by a severe stroke, losing much of the function of his right side. With strong resolve and support from family and colleagues, he fought the debilitation while, with the assistance of younger associates, he recorded his physical struggle and progress on video tape. Though partially impaired, Murray made remarkable strides, and in spite of his difficulties, remained vibrant working his craft.

Reflecting upon the Kennedy assassination of 1963 and its place in contemporary society, Murray comments:

We might have recovered from Kennedy's assassination. Oswald's murder was even more traumatic. I think many people would rather believe it *was* a conspiracy, than live

with unanswerable questions that arose from that awful weekend. It shattered all our lives, and we keep looking for some sort of *logic* to explain it. Our minds rebel against senseless events and try to give them some order – something that will tie up the loose ends into a neat package. We're really not so different from primitive tribes who believe a bolt of lightning *must* have been an event planned by someone all-powerful.

Obviously, no single person can disprove all the fictions that have worked their way into the assassination folklore. But, thanks to my photos, I've had a unique opportunity to see how so-called "researchers" will bend the truth when there's a buck to be made. They're corrupting History, and it's shameful.

I don't accept all the Warren Commission details, but I think their main conclusion was basically correct. For those who care enough to examine it, Oswald left a trail of irrational, violent behavior since he was a child. We'll probably never find answers that cover all the unknowables. But there have been many who have built profitable careers exploiting the doubts that exist. In this Talk Show culture, facts don't stand much of a chance against lies–or a $40-million film budget.

Lately I've decided that a person's response to the Kennedy assassination theories is a good litmus test of their judgment on other matters. It's like we're being asked to choose our own paranoia. Depending on which book you read last, it was either the Mafia or the Military Industrial Complex or the CIA – or was it pro-Castro Cubans or anti-Castro Cubans. Who's next? Meanwhile, the most reasonable thesis is being buried under all the lies. And *History* is the big loser.[40]

CHAPTER NOTES

1. Murray interviews, 11/22/1985; 10/24/1992; Letter, Murray to Trask, 10/19/1992; Copy of WBAP-TV film and out-takes in the possession of Murray. Unless specifically noted, all other information in this chapter is taken from these Murray interviews, a letter of 10/19/1992 and Trask telephone interview with Murray, 8/26/1996.
2. Letter, Murray to Trask, 8/6/1986.
3. Murray telephone interview, 3/27/1986.
4. Harry Cabluck bus photographs #1-2, 11/22/1963.
5. Murray photographs, roll 1, #1-3, 11/22/1963; Josiah Thompson, *Six Seconds in Dallas*, p. 135.
6. Murray photographs, roll 1, #4-7, 11/22/1963; Notes on reverse of oversize print of Murray photograph roll 1, #7, located within the Richard Sprague collection, Western New England College, Springfield, Massachusetts. Subsequent photo descriptions come from an examination of eight contact sheets and numerous prints obtained from Murray of his photo take of 11/22/1963. Frame numbers will not be specifically mentioned unless they are particularly noteworthy.
7. *Hearings Before the President's Commission on the Assassination of President Kennedy*, v. 7, p. 546.
8. Ibid., v. 6, p. 252.
9. J. Gary Shaw, *Cover-up*, p. 72. Hugh Betzner, Jr, seen at left in roll 1, #17-18 later deposed at the sheriff's office that, "These police officers and the man in plain clothes were digging around in the dirt as if they were looking for a bullet." (*Hearings*, v. 24, p. 200). Betzner is also photographed by Murray at the Sheriff's office in roll 3, #15.
10. *Hearings*, op. cit., v. 6, p. 252; Mark A. Oakes, *Eyewitness Video Tape*, Foster interview, 7/9/1991.
11. Trask telephone interview with William Allen, 1/20/1987.
12. *Hearings*, op. cit., v. 5, p. 111-112; v. 26, p. 497; Mark Oakes, "On the Trail of the Mystery FBI Man," *Dateline: Dallas*, Winter 1993, p. 31-32; Todd Vaughan interview, 10/24/1992; Jim Garrison, *On the Trail of the Assassins*, p. 209; Murray photographs, roll 1, #16, 17, 19, 11/22/1963.
13. *Cover-up*, op. cit., p. 14-18, 26-28.
14. A close inspection of Murray photograph, roll 1, #21 reveals four civilians around the sewer cover looking or touching the ground. Across Elm Street a clump of people stand near the knoll steps. Officer Foster is next to a civilian, James Tague, who is pointing toward the triple underpass. Tague had a nick and some blood on his cheek and told Foster and Deputy Walters that that location was his position when he felt a sting on his face during the assassination. A crowd is meanwhile radiating to the front of the Book Depository building.
15. *Hearings*, v. 7, p. 310-313, 315-320; v. 16, p. 963.
16. Mark Lane, *Rush to Judgment*,. p. 348-349; Letter, Willis to Trask, 6/29/1984; Trask interview with Willis, 11/22/1984.
17. Jim Murray photograph, roll 1, #25 & #27, 11/22/1963. Since my original publication of this discovery in 1994, I have found the same non-Ruby man in two other photographic sources. In May 1996 I was requested by CBS News to review the so-called Cooper film containing preserved film clips originally shot by cameramen from Fort Worth's KTVT television station. While reviewing the film with CBS News anchor Dan Rather, I noted a brief clip showing this man at the northeast corner of the Book Depository at a time when Amos Euins was being escorted by Sergeant Harkness. When asked on-camera to comment upon the identity of this man, I stated that along with the evidence of the Willis and Murray photos, "I think it's safe to say that this is the man in the other two pictures, who is not Jack Ruby." In 1997 while reviewing tape of film shot by Dallas television station WFAA cameramen, I located this same non-Ruby man in a clip taken in front of the Book Depository at a time when eyewitness Howard Brennan was being escorted from the front door area.
18. Howard L. Brennan, *Eyewitness To History*, p. 17.
19. Letter, Murray to Trask, 4/1/1986.
20. Letter, Murray to Trask, 5/17/1996; Letter, Murray to Trask, 6/10/1997. Knowing how such relatively innocuous events can be made into conspiratorial flights of fancy by some researchers, Murray did not freely recount this incident to the author until some years after his first interview.
21. Letter, Murray to Trask, 4/1/1986.
22. Murray photographs, roll 8, #8-14. Larry Schiller went on to have an interesting and varied career. Phasing out of photojournalism work, he was successful as an entrepreneur, collaborator, ghost writer, writer, director and producer. He set up an audio taping of the hospital statement of Jack Ruby in 1966, worked in movies and television earning an academy award and several emmies, began a long collaboration with Norman Mailer in 1973 including on his 1993 book, *Oswald's Tale,* and was intimately connected to the O. J. Simpson case in the late 1990s. As many would say about him, "He's there wherever things were happening."
23. Murray photograph, roll 8, #16; James P. Hosty, Jr., *Assignment: Oswald*, p. 20-23, 29, 59-60.
24. Murray photographs, roll 7, #3-13; roll 8, #17-23; Bill Lord interview of James Chaney for WFAA-TV, 11/22/1963.
25. Murray photographs, roll 7, #14-18; roll 8, #24-26; *Hearings*, v.7, p. 278-285, 288. The palm prints made at this time are replicated in *Hearings*, v. 17, p. 510-511. It is marked "Printed 11/22/63 in Capt. Fritz's office. JBHicks-JCDay." Another set of hand prints are reproduced in the same volume on p. 283-284. It appears that the card containing fingerprints alluded too in the next text paragraph is not replicated in the fingerprint reproductions found in *Hearings*, v. 17.
26. Letter, Murray to Trask, 7/11/1993.
27. Letter, Murray to Trask, 6/20/1996; Letter, Murray to Trask, 6/10/1997; Murray photographs, roll 7, #24-26.
28. Letter, Murray to Trask, 9/3/1996; Letter, 7/11/1993; Murray photographs, roll 7, #27-34; roll 8, # 35.
29. *LIFE*, November 29, 1963, p. 3, 38; Gerald R. Ford, *Portrait of the Assassin*, dust jacket.
30. Murray photograph, roll 8, #36.
31. Letter, 7/11/1993.
32. Letter, Murray to Trask, 1/2/1997; *Hearings*, op. cit., v. 13, p. 9; v. 21, p. 205, 209, 223; Charles A. Crenshaw, *JFK: Conspiracy of Silence*, p. 182-184; Murray photographs, frame #13-16, 11/24/1963.
33. Letter, 1/2/1997.
34. Ibid.; *Hearings*, op. cit., v. 21, p. 435; v. 25, p. 174; Seth Kantor, *Who Was Jack Ruby?*, p. 51-53; Murray photographs of billboard, frame #31.
35. Letter, Murray to Trask, 2/26/1997; *LIFE*, 12/ 6/1963; *LIFE, John F. Kennedy Memorial Edition*, p. [64-65]
36. Letter; 2/26/1997: *EPOCA Numero Speciale in Memoria di Kennedy*, 11/22/1964, p. 62-63, 119, 127.
37. *Six Seconds*, op. cit., p. 125, 135, 246.
38. Ibid., p. 246.
39. Letter, 7/11/1993; Letter, Murray to Trask, 8/15/1993; Letter, Murray to Trask, 6/10/1997.
40. Ibid.

INDEX

THAT DAY IN DALLAS

has been published in an edition of sewn, soft-cover copies.
Designed by Ethel and Richard B. Trask,
the text was composed in Times New Roman
and printed by Thomson-Shore, Inc., on
Fortune Matte, acid-free paper.

Richard B. Trask is Archivist for the town of Danvers, Massachusetts. He is an acknowledged expert on the 1692 Salem witchcraft outbreak, and has appeared in numerous documentaries on the subject. He is author of the recent book, *The Devil Hath Been Raised,* and is curator of the historic Rebecca Nurse Homestead. His interest in the Kennedy assassination began at age 16 in 1963, and his 1994 volume *Pictures of the Pain: Photography and the Assassination of President Kennedy* is acknowledged as a classic study. He has been consulted by the Assassination Records Review Board and CBS News, and has authored a booklet for the Sixth Floor Museum in Dallas, Texas. He and his wife Ethel are partners in Yeoman Press, and live in their restored 17th century home with their daughter Elizabeth.